CHRISTIAN COUNTER-ATTACK

CHRISTIAN
COUNTER-ATTACK

By

ARNOLD LUNN

and

GARTH LEAN

LONDON

BLANDFORD PRESS

Acknowledgements

Acknowledgements to the publishers of books from whom we have quoted and page references to sources are to be found at the end of each chapter.

First published September 1969

© 1969 Blandford Press Ltd
167 High Holborn, London WC1

Printed in Great Britain by
Northumberland Press Limited
Gateshead

CONTENTS

Introduction   1

Part One: THE RETREAT FROM CHRISTIANITY

1 CHRISTENDOM IN CRISIS   11
2 'THE PERFUME OF AN EMPTY VASE'   17
3 PERMISSIVE STORM-TROOPERS   25
4 THE PRO-POT LOBBY   35
5 THE 'AFFECTLESS SOCIETY'?   47
6 STUDENT VIOLENCE   57
7 IS HUMANISM AN ALTERNATIVE?   70
8 THE EXPLOITATION OF BONHOEFFER   77

Part Two: COUNTER-ATTACK

9   THE CONFLICT BETWEEN SCIENCE AND
    MATERIALISM   93
10 WHY CHRISTIANITY SURVIVED   110
11 AN APOLOGY FOR APOLOGETICS   117
12 FAITH BY EXPERIMENT   138
13 COMMITMENT FOR COUNTER-ATTACK   150
14 THE COMPLETE REVOLUTION   160
15 A JOB WAITING TO BE DONE   168
    Index   174

'There are frontiersmen and frontiersmen of course. There is what one might call the Munich school, who will always sell the pass in the belief that their position can be more happily defended from foothills to the rear. Such people are not commonly seen as apologists. They are reckoned to be New Theologians. They are too busy learning from their enemies to do much in defence of their friends. The typical apologist is a man whose every dyke is his last ditch. He will carry the war into the enemy's country; he will yield not an inch of his own.'

DR AUSTIN FARRER from his chapter 'The Christian Apologist' in *Light on C. S. Lewis* (Geoffrey Bles, 1965), p. 23.

Introduction

Observers as diverse as Professor Mascall and Mr Philip Toynbee, to mention only two, have attributed the declining influence of Christianity in recent years, in large measure, to a failure of nerve on the part of Christians. A striking example of this is the acceptance by many Christians that the only case which is better for not being stated is the case for Christianity. No political party or commercial firm would dream of adopting so ridiculous an attitude. Christianity itself conquered the Roman world because its missionaries were not only prepared to die, if necessary, for their faith but were passionately anxious to persuade men that Jesus of Nazareth had proved His deity by rising from the dead; and in our own day, Communists have conquered much of the globe because the majority of Communists all over the world welcome the opportunity to state the case for Communism. The theory that you actually damage your case by stating it was left to Christians to develop.

This theory is, of course, not new. John Wesley, in his *Journal* for 8 June 1741, described how he took the advice of such theorists during a coach journey from London to Leicester. 'For these two days,' he wrote, 'I made an experiment which I had been so often and earnestly pressed to do – speaking to none about the things of God, unless my heart was free to it. But what was the event? Why, (1) That I spoke to none at all for fourscore miles together; no, not even to him that travelled with me in the chaise, unless a few words at first setting out. (2) That I had no cross either to bear, or to take up, and, in an hour or two, fell fast asleep. (3) That I had much respect shown me wherever I came, everyone behaving to me as to a civil, good-natured gentleman. Oh how pleasing is all this to flesh and blood! Need ye "compass sea and land" to make proselytes to this?'

The world now, as in Wesley's day, is ready to tolerate the Christian who is content, as he emerges from the Christian ghetto, to behave as 'a civil and good-natured gentleman' who is indeed too gentlemanly to mention the radical points of difference between his beliefs and those of his secular friends. And it is because many, but by no means all, Christians, have accepted this convention that any discussion of Christianity with non-Christians is a solecism, whereas it is natural and reasonable for anti-Christians to engage in anti-Christian propaganda.

It is the common experience of many, as indeed both authors of this book have verified in their own lives, that if a Christian comes to be known as a man who positively welcomes a discussion of Christianity a surprising number of people will open the subject with him – some because they are genuinely interested in discovering any real evidence for the supernatural and others because they hope that the Christianity, which they have yet to try, might provide an answer to their own personal difficulties, or to the problems of society. And in this connection we wish to emphasize a point which will be made later in this book. There is no single remedy for the decline of Christianity. Different people have different vocations. Many have been converted by the example of Christians the sanctity of whose lives and whose devoted care of the poor, and the handicapped, provide the kind of evidence which speaks louder than any words. Christianity again owes an immense debt to all the uncounted thousands of Christians doing a quiet job which attracts little or no attention. Of all this we are well aware but we none the less believe that the revival of Christianity depends, among other things, on a great increase of what may be called lay missionaries in what is now essentially a mission country.

Arnold Lunn is a Catholic and Garth Lean is an Anglican. Both of us are convinced that the beliefs which we share are infinitely, yes infinitely, more important than those on which we differ, and furthermore that the points on which we differ are far less important than the difference between Christians who make some effort to change the world and those who seem mainly concerned to change Christianity so as to make it more acceptable to the world.

In this book, we first briefly examine the position of Christianity in today's world and show that the Victorian atheists who believed that the Christian code would survive the abandonment of the Christian creed have been proved wrong by events. An examination of the way in which the erosion of that code is producing a violent and callous society invites the conclusion that a revival of Christianity is necessary if society is to be reborn or civilization is to survive. But this will not come about if, as many maintain, science has disproved the God hypothesis and if Christianity has been shown to be untrue. Arnold Lunn, in two signed chapters, demonstrates why both these theses are irrational and, in a third, draws on his long experience as a Christian apologist to describe the methods whereby people as unlikely as the late Professor Joad and the Communist Louis Budenz were brought to Christian belief. Garth Lean, in his signed chapters, outlines an experimental approach to faith which has led thousands to an experience of Christian reality, and suggests what he conceives to be some essential prerequisites to any major awakening. While each of us is responsible only for those portions of the book which are signed by himself, we are each in broad agreement with each other's approach in the chapters signed by the other. Each takes his illustrations from his own experience, fully realizing that others could produce examples no less relevant.

We do not believe that the current attempts to induce a revival through ecumenism or the restructuring of Church organization, necessary as each of these is, will, of themselves, have the desired effect. Dr Bryan Wilson sees ecumenism as a sign of, and response to, weakness. 'Since progress cannot be made in converting society,' he wrote, 'the Churches might enjoy the appearance of success by converting one another. Even if men are not being saved, if God is less worshipped and society unredeemed, at least the church might be saved, and the clergy might redeem faded reputations.' We ourselves believe in a militant, as distinct from a defeatist, ecumenism, a fighting alliance of all Christians which, as we wrote in *The New Morality*, 'will carry the battle into the materialist camp and expect a change in multitudes of human lives which will affect social, national and international situations.' 'Love men. Slay errors,' wrote St Augustine. Ecumenists must not only pray together. They must also slay together.

The Rev. Nicholas Stacey maintains that a 'mammoth structural stripping down' of the Church, to match what he calls the 'theological strip-tease' being conducted by his former colleagues on the South Bank of the Thames, could lead to a 'resurrected Church'.

There is much to be said for the employment of

more flexible tactics in the winning of men and for our efforts to be less tied to the maintenance of buildings and organizational frameworks; but one wonders whether the premise from which Mr Stacey argues – his 'failure' as Rector of Woolwich where he and 'one of the largest and ablest teams of clergy in England' 'played every card in the pack' and 'achieved virtually not one of the modest things we hoped for' – is the best starting point for the strategy of a resurrected church. 'These have been the most dramatic and exhausting years of my life,' he wrote in his much publicized article 'A Mission's Failure'. 'We have laughed and occasionally wept. We have tried to pray and to love. We have been brazen as a Dean Street publicity agent – in the early stages I pulled a beauty queen on a vegetable barrow through the main shopping street. . . . We have raised a fortune and spent it. We have quite obviously failed.' Mr Stacey may have played every card in *his* pack, but he might, one feels, have tried a different pack before departing into Oxfam, an excellent, but essentially secular, body.

Christians are delighted to be associated with such good causes as are approved by our secular society, the attack, for instance, on racialism, but too few of us defy fashion by protesting against the persecution of Christians behind the Iron Curtain, for instance, or by offering some opposition to the revolt against traditional morality.

Again our intimidated Christians are influenced by the democratic criterion of truth, the illusion that the case for Christianity has been weakened because Christianity no longer commands a majority in countries once Christian. We should, of course, be proclaiming that the *consequences* of the Christian decline provide indirect evidence for Christianity.

It was, we think, Kierkegaard who predicted that 'Christianity may be taken away from Europe as the only way of convincing people of its truth'. An effective counter-attack on the secularists will not overlook the realistic predictions of Christians who foresaw the consequences of repudiating God and the fatuous inanities of such Utopian secularists as Herbert Spencer, who is quoted by Dean Inge (*Outspoken Essays*, p. 163) as follows: 'Progress is not an accident but a necessity. What we call evil and immorality must disappear. It is certain that man must become perfect.' 'For every 100,000 of the population 66 years ago there were 250 crimes,' wrote Eric Clark in *The Observer* (18 September 1960), 'last year there were 2,374.' Herbert Spencer's successors would not agree that this tenfold increase of crime since he predicted the inevitable perfectibility of man was due to the repudiation of Christianity, but it has certainly coincided with the increasing secularization of society.

In his introduction to *A History of Modern Thought*, published by 'The Home University Library' in 1913, just before the first World War, Professor J. B. Bury wrote: 'The struggle of reason against authority has ended in what appears to be a decisive and permanent victory for liberty. In the most civilized and progressive countries freedom of discussion is recognized as a fundamental principle.' None of those who shared the professor's naïve illusions could have suspected the remote possibility that Germany, which was then 'civilized and progressive', could degenerate into Nazism, and most of them welcomed the Soviet Russia which emerged from the first World War as a great advance on Tsarist Russia. No such progressive foresaw in 1913 that more people would be liquidated for political heresies and racial background in the 'progressive' twentieth century than had been liquidated for religious heresies in any previous century.

We have been lamentably slow to make use in our counter-attack of the results which have followed in Russia from the adoption of atheism as the State philosophy. Catholics, to take one example, are brought up on Galileo, but whereas no scientist was ever executed for his scientific views by the Church, many scientists have been imprisoned and some liquidated because they did not accept Stalin's doctrines of orthodox Lamarkian evolution. Details of this persecution will be found in Chapter II.

Dogmatic atheism has had its day. Its successor is nihilism, and nihilism apparently is news. That some students should have demanded a free supply of contraceptives and the abolition of examinations, is not particularly disturbing, for the extravagances of thought are characteristic of youth and an undergraduate society could have a great deal of fun debating such a motion as 'A Bachelor of Tarts should be substituted for a Bachelor of Arts'. But that such absurdities should be considered worth reporting in responsible papers is disquieting.

Orthodoxy, of course, is not news. Traditionalists tend to react with mute disgust against the much publicized absurdities of *avant-garde* clerics who try to come to terms with the modern world, clerics whose propaganda has been caricatured as an attempt to compromise on the agreement that fornication is to be regarded as unchristian in Lent, and it is perhaps only those who attack with vigour the appeasers within Christianity who fully realize what immense potential support already exists for an uncompromising counter-attack on the atheism, admitted or camouflaged, which is destroying the Western world.　　　A.L.

　　　　　　　　　　　　　　　　　　G.D.L.

REFERENCES

DR BRYAN WILSON: 'The Churches' Last Hope', *The Observer*, 9 October 1966

THE REV. NICHOLAS STACEY: 'How the Church Could Survive', *The Observer*, 23 May 1965; 'A Mission's Failure', *The Observer*, 6 December 1964

ECUMENISM – Militant or Defeatist: *The New Morality* by Arnold Lunn and Garth Lean (Blandford Press). Revised and enlarged edition, March 1967, pp. 186–190.

Part One

THE RETREAT FROM CHRISTIANITY

I

Christendom in Crisis

Lord Reith, the creator and the first Director-General of the British Broadcasting Corporation, was asked on television where he found the 'certainty and the self-confidence' which enabled him to exercise the 'incredible authority' of that office. He replied: 'I just felt I could – mark you, with the help of the Almighty, and I say that seriously – I could do whatever was required. I would say that the Almighty was there in my receiving that job and was there in the execution of it.'

A few days earlier, the Reith Lecturer for 1967, Dr Edmund Leach, the Provost of King's College, Cambridge, declared that 'men have become like gods and should behave as such'.

This contrast between confidence in Almighty God and confidence in Almighty Man is, perhaps, the most fundamental of all the differences between the world of sixty years ago and the world of today. One may question whether Lord Reith's confidence rested primarily in God or in himself just as one may suspect that Dr Leach may be less sure of man's excellence than his words imply, but the fact remains that sixty years ago, when Lord Reith was growing to manhood in his father's manse, it was still intellectually respectable to believe that God was wiser than man and that He could intervene in human affairs. Now it is modish to assume that man has come of age and can do very well on his own. The intellectual *avant-garde* assumes that God is dead, and at least one school of theologians appears to agree with them.

This change in intellectual fashion has led many to ask whether Christianity is capable of revival – or even of survival. And, in fact, Christianity does seem to have steadily declined in influence in the sixty years under scrutiny. In the years before the first world war, it was the dominant creed of the Establishment and of ordinary people throughout Europe, including Russia, in America and in almost every other developed nation. It was, in addition, the official religion of the authorities in the European empires in Asia and Africa, and the subject of a vast and seemingly successful missionary effort in China and elsewhere. Today, on the other hand, atheism is the official religion in the Communist third of the world, and the newly independent countries of Asia and Africa have tended to turn away from the religion of their former rulers. In Indonesia and in some parts of South America, it is true, there are at the moment large-scale movements towards Christianity, but in the Sudan, Pakistan and elsewhere Christian missionaries have been expelled, and K. M. Panikkar, the Indian historian and diplomat, heads a chapter in his monumental *Asia and Western Dominance* with the bald statement, 'The Failure of Christian Missions'. 'It will hardly be denied,' he writes, 'that in spite of the immense and sustained effort made by the churches with the support of the lay public in the European countries and America, the attempt to conquer Asia for Christ has definitely failed.'

More serious still is the decline of Christian influence in those countries which were the bases from which this missionary work was conducted. All the

Protestant Churches of Europe now record a shrink-age of membership, of conversions and of candidates for ordination. Church attendance varies from 3 per cent of the population in Stockholm to about 14 per cent in England, a figure inflated by the larger pro-portion of Catholics in the English population. A series of articles in *The Times*, under the heading 'Christians Asleep', concluded that 'it is difficult to avoid the feeling that the Church of England is on the brink of crisis'. 'It is, in a rather frightening way, a microcosm of British society – unsure of its position, reluctant and ill-equipped to keep pace with a changing environment and internally divided to a point where sectarian interests are allowed to out-weigh the common good.' The Bishop of London commented on this conclusion, 'We may think this or that statement is wrong or unfair, but if the Church of England looks like that to an outside observer we cannot ignore the criticism.' A prominent English Dean told one of us, 'We are conducting a holding action, and hardly even that.'

In America, the figures are startlingly different. Church attendance is said to stand at 57 per cent of the population, and church membership at 63 per cent, a point to which the figures have grown steadily over sixty years. 'Yet no one,' comments Dr Bryan Wilson in his *Religion in Secular Society*, 'is prepared to suggest America is other than a secularized country. . . . It would require an ingenious sociological analysis to show that the development of American society was materially affected by its high rate of church-goings or that of Sweden by its very low rate.'

Dr Wilson concludes that church membership in the United States owes much to status-seeking and to the churches' part in the social life of immigrant ethnic groups. He maintains that 'though religious practice has increased, the vacuousness of popular religious ideas has also increased: the content and meaning of religious commitment has been acculturated'.

Those who listened to the inauguration of President Nixon may doubt whether such a cynical explanation is wholly adequate. Yet few would quarrel with the Jesuit theologian, John Courtney Murray, who, while maintaining that America is still a God-fearing nation, points to the 'atheism of distraction' where people are 'just too damn busy' to worry about God. 'The great American proposition,' he writes, 'is "religion is good for the kids though I'm not religious myself!"'

A Gallup Poll recorded in the *Daily Telegraph* of 25 May 1968 found that 60 per cent of Americans believe that religion is losing its influence in daily life, whereas in 1957 only 14 per cent held this view. 'The shrinking influence, of the Church,' the paper reported, 'is attributed to increasing violence and crime; to the Church not keeping up with the times; and the Church becoming too involved in social and political issues.'

The Catholic Church, for long the Federal Reserve Bank of the faith, has its own troubles. Pope Paul himself has stated that 'a spirit of corrosive criticism has become fashionable in certain sections of Catholic life', and the Paulist Father Thomas Stransky, an official of the Secretariat for Christian Unity in Rome, suggests that the Church is suffering from 'a silent schism' of rebels who are remaining Catholic in name but are 'hanging loose' from the institutional church. 'This year alone,' writes *Time* Magazine on 22 November 1968, 'at least 463 Catholic clerics in the U.S. have left the priesthood, many of them to marry.'

It is, in fact, hard to dissent from Dr Bryan Wilson's

conclusion that men in the West 'act less and less from religious motivation' and that the Churches, once the 'arbiters of moral behaviour', have 'surrendered the claim of religion to guide the course of social policy, the decisions of statesmen, the operation of social institutions, and, latterly, even the everyday behaviour of the man-in-the-street.'

At the same time, there is little evidence that ordinary people are unwilling to believe in God. In 1965, the American pollster, Mr Lou Harris, recorded that '97 per cent of the American people said they believe in God' and the ABC Gallup Poll of September 1965 put the equivalent number in Britain at 84 per cent. It is, apparently, from the so-called intellectual classes that the initiative has come for what the Princeton theologian, Dr Paul Ramsay, describes as 'the first attempt in recorded history to build a culture upon the premise that God is dead'.

It is maintained that these intellectuals have been forced to their conclusions by the findings of science. 'Secularization, science, urbanization – all have made it comparatively easy,' wrote *Time* (8 April 1966) 'for modern man to ask where God is, and hard for the man of faith to give a convincing answer, even to himself . . . Is God dead? It is a question which tantalizes both believers, who perhaps secretly fear that he is, and atheists who possibly suspect that the answer is no.'

Before we investigate the claim that science has made the God hypothesis untenable or that modern men can no longer honestly believe in Christianity, we will examine the godless culture of which Dr Ramsay speaks. Is it, in fact, living up to the hopes of its atheist pioneers?

REFERENCES

LORD REITH: Television interviews with Malcolm Muggeridge, reprinted in *The Listener*, 30 November and 7 and 14 December 1967.

DR EDMUND LEACH: The Reith Lectures, 1967, reprinted in *The Listener*, starting 16 November 1967.

K. M. PANIKKAR: 'Asia and Western Dominance' (Allen & Unwin, 1953), pp. 454–7.

'CHRISTIANS ASLEEP': A series of six articles in *The Times* (18 to 25 May 1966) by a Staff reporter. The Bishop of London's comment was in *The Times* on 7 June.

DR BRYAN WILSON: Religion in Secular Society (C. A. Watts, 1966) pp. 2, 89, xii, 98, x, 65, 77.

TIME MAGAZINE: 'Is God Dead?' (8 April 1966), from which quotations from the Rev. John Murray, S.J., and Dr Paul Ramsay are taken.

'Catholic Freedom *v*. Authority' (22 November 1968) from which the quotations from Pope Paul and Father Stransky are taken.

For Catholicism in the U.S.A. also see 'An English Catholic Tours the U.S.' by Sir Arnold Lunn (*National Review*, 24 January 1967), being reflections on his 18th lecture tour in America.

2

'The Perfume of an Empty Vase'

Many of the great Heresiarchs of the Victorian era, who rejected the Christian creed, continued to be influenced by the Christian code and bitterly resented the prediction that the code would not long survive the creed on which it was based.

T. H. Huxley, the eminent scientist who invented the word 'agnostic' to describe his state of mind, was a strict moralist. 'If some Great Power would agree to make me always think what is true and do what is right, on condition of being turned into a sort of clock and wound up every morning before I got out of bed,' he once wrote, 'I would instantly close with the offer.'

As a member of the London School Board from 1870-1872, he insisted on the need for moral education. He supported the reading of the Bible as the basis of such education, agreeing that in this way 'children will be taught the truths of the Christian life and conduct which we all desire they should know'. He opposed those who wished to abolish 'religious' teaching in order to get rid of theology, because this would be like 'burning the ship to get rid of the cockroaches'.

Huxley would have preferred a scientific approach as a better method of teaching the ethical system on which all were broadly agreed, but believed this to be impracticable in the then state of education among the masses. He, himself, however, rejected the supernatural and looked forward confidently to the day when the scientific method could be applied universally.

'I see no limit,' he said in his final statement of belief, the Romanes Lecture delivered in Oxford in 1893, 'to the extent to which intelligence and will, guided by sound principles of investigation, and organized in common effort, may modify the conditions of existence, for periods longer than now covered by history. And much may be done to change the nature of man himself. The intelligence which has converted the brother of the wolf into the faithful guardian of the flock, ought to be able to do something towards curbing the instincts of savagery in civilized man.'

Renan, the French philosopher, who started life in St Sulpice seminary where he lost his faith, thought otherwise. 'It is possible,' he wrote, 'that the collapse of supernatural belief will be followed by the collapse of moral convictions and that the moment when humanity sees the reality of things will mark a real moral decline. We are living on the perfume of an empty vase.' Few objective observers today will doubt that Renan's prediction was more accurate than Huxley's.

This is not to say that moral rectitude is the monopoly of Theists in general or of Christians in particular. Whereas many who have not rejected the Christian creed make little attempt to practise the Christian code, many others practise that code who have long since rejected Christianity itself. But in society as a whole, the decline in Christian faith and in morality have proceeded simultaneously.

A study of the literature of the West in the decades since Huxley's death, confirms this view. The distinguished literary critic, Cyril Connolly, in his survey

*The Modern Movement: 100 Key Books from Eng-
land, France and America, 1880-1950* makes this
abundantly clear. His survey, which was undertaken
for the *Sunday Times* and subsequently published
in book form, involved the choosing as key books 'those
which best illustrated the spirit of the modern movement which dawned with Flaubert and Baudelaire,
reached its zenith early in the century and only became
past history in the fifties – if it has become past
history'.

Mr Connolly assumes that the Modern Movement is
in essence 'humanist'. Some Christians, it is true,
appear in his list, but he excludes such 'traditionalists' as Chesterton, Belloc and Kipling as much for
their beliefs as for their techniques, and attributes
the 'petering out' of the Movement to secession of too
many writers from 'humanism'. Eliot, Edith Sitwell,
Waugh and Auden are among those he mentions as
seceding to 'the religious fold'. He defines the 'twin
features' of the movement as 'faith in the intellect as
destroyer of pretences and illusions, as man's true
guide wherever it may lead, and the equally strong
belief in the validity of the imagination, the enlarge-
ment of sensibility, the Côté Voltaire and the Côté
Rousseau . . .'

So it is fair to say that Mr Connolly's key books are,
in general, representative of the modern atheist spirit
– and that their tone and content are important evidence of whether Huxley or Renan was right in their
opposing views of the dependence of the Christian
ethical system upon Christian faith. It is instructive,
therefore, to read the assessment of the distinguished
American critic, Joseph Wood Krutch, formerly Professor of English at Columbia University, that 'though
his (Mr Connolly's) list does include certain works
which are neither beatnik, sadistic, existential, nor

sexually perverse, at least a half – and perhaps two-thirds – of them might, I think, be classified as guide-posts to perdition' (*Saturday Review*, 6 May 1967). A study of Mr Connolly's brilliant notes on each of his hundred books confirms the accuracy of Mr Krutch's classification.

The word perdition is taken from a saying by one of Mr Connolly's key authors, Guillaume Apollinaire, the champion successively of Cubism, Dadaism and Surrealism, whom Mr Connolly describes as 'novelist, gourmet, bibliophile and pornocrat'. The quotation from which it is taken appears on the monument to Apollinaire recently unveiled by the French Minister of Culture, André Malraux. It reads: 'We have set out as pilgrims whose destination is perdition . . . across streets, across countries, and across reason itself.' Here is an echo of the lines from Baudelaire, as translated by Robert Lowell, in which Mr Connolly finds the quintessence of modernity:

> Only when we drink poison are we well –
> We want, this fire so burns our brain tissue,
> To drown in the abyss – heaven or hell.
> Who cares? Through the unknown we'll find
> the new.

Guillaume Apollinaire was an admirer of the Marquis de Sade, whom he described as 'the freest spirit which ever existed'. He predicted that de Sade's would be the dominant influence of the twentieth century – 'a prophecy', comments Mr Krutch, 'which seems in the course of being fulfilled'.

Mr Krutch thinks it still unlikely that an American Minister of Arts, if one existed, would publicly honour a poet with Apollinaire's views. He continues:

But if we are not yet quite up to the French in this

respect, there is no doubt that the avant-garde, even when perverse and sadistic, is no longer without honour even in rather surprising quarters, and that mass-circulation magazines give frequent and extensive treatment to movies, plays, novels and poems which in one way or another – extravagant concern with usual abnormal sexuality, violence, cruelty, or at least the nihilism of the absurd – seem to be headed along the road which Apollinaire bids them take.

After analysing the reaction of popular magazines to a conspicuous American novel (James Baldwin's *Another Country*), a conspicuous movie (*The Naked Prey*) and a conspicuous English play (John Osborne's *A Bond Honoured*), and the work of two high-brow American critics, Leslie Fielder and Susan Sontag, Dr Krutch concludes:

I suppose that anyone who undertook to trace the development of modernism would have to begin by asking whether or not there is a single dominating characteristic of this latest development, any one which, at least by its frequent emphasis, seems to distinguish contemporary modernism from the movement out of which it is said to have grown. True, this modernism does indeed seem to be compounded of many simplicities and not all who represent it include all of them in their mixtures. Thus one distinguishing characteristic is the tendency to elevate raw sexual experience to a position of supreme importance so that the Quest for the Holy Grail becomes a quest for the perfect orgasm. Other characteristics are homosexuality, nihilism, and that impulse to self-destructions typified in the cult of drugs. Still another is that taste for violence which, as in the case of Baldwin, becomes un-mistakably sadistic. If I had to answer the question 'What is most fundamental?' I should be inclined to say 'the taste for violence'. The belief that violence is the only appropriate response to an absurd world is the one element most often present in any individual's special version of the moment's avant-gardism.

Mr Connolly states that the Modern Movement began with 'a revolt against the bourgeois in France, the Victorians in England, the Puritanism and materialism of America'. 'The modern spirit,' he continues, 'was a combination of certain intellectual qualities inherited from the Enlightenment: lucidity, irony, skepticism, intellectual curiosity, combined with the passionate intensity and enhanced sensibility of the Romantics, their rebellion and sense of technical experiment, their awareness of living in a tragic age.'

All this is true enough, but it does not explain why the unique characteristics of avant-gardism are not the characteristics of the Enlightenment or of any romanticism except that commonly called decadent. 'How,' asks Dr Krutch, 'do lucidity, irony, skepticism or even intellectual curiosity become preludes to the "century of de Sade"?'

Perhaps the answer can be found in the reflections of Dr Will Durant, the American historian and philosopher, who confirms that most of Western literature and social philosophy, after 1950, was 'the voice of freedom against authority, of the child against the parent, of the pupil against the teacher, of man against the state'. He continues:

Through many years . . . I shared in that individualistic revolt. I do not regret the rebellion . . . but I wonder whether the battle I fought was not too completely won. Have we too much freedom? Have we so long ridiculed authority in the family, discipline in education, rules in art, decency in conduct, and law in the state that our liberation has brought us close to chaos in the family and the school, in morals, arts, ideas, and government?

Miss Pamela Hansford Johnson, in her book, *On Iniquity*, goes deeper:

When the Sermon on the Mount was bundled into the dustbin (or indeed, any code of ideas that had raised men's eyes from the ground) a moral vacuum was created: and the liberal humanists have not succeeded in filling it. . . . They have been unable to offer an alternative faith to the one they have renounced, except for faith in the beneficial effects of total permissiveness in every form of culture. This faith is a romantic one, even more romantic than Rousseau's. Once they ceased to believe even in the possibility of sheer iniquity and replaced this by a belief in Freud, they tore up the very stones of self-discipline and moral responsibility . . .

So, as Renan predicted, the rejection of the Christian creed has been accompanied by the abandonment of the Christian ethic, and the resulting sense of nihilism has penetrated widely through the nations. For, as Malraux himself remarked, 'In a universe without God, life is absurd'.

NOTE

Fifty Works of English Literature Which We Could Do Without:
Further evidence of the theme of this chapter is provided by this book by Miss Brigid Brophy, the high priestess of British 'humanism', her husband, Mr Michael Levy, and Mr Charles Osborne,

Assistant Literary Director of the Arts Council. Their collective literary judgements are eccentric – *Hamlet* is 'over-rated', the Wessex novels 'silly' and Shaw's *St Joan* 'insipid', to take only three instances – but it soon becomes apparent that their real complaint against the authors about whom they write is that they were not 'enlightened' twentieth-century intellectuals like themselves. They say that Scott is 'barely educated', Gerard Manley Hopkins is a 'mental cripple' and Wordsworth a 'Philistine'. A dozen authors are written off because they were Christians, while fifteen or so are considered too sexually inexperienced to be taken seriously. Mark Twain is 'clean and sexless', Lewis Carroll 'humourless' and unconsciously 'kinky', George Moore 'exemplary', Sheridan 'prudish' and so on. In their introduction they state that the Bible only escaped being on their list of unwanted books by being a translation and therefore outside their terms of reference.

REFERENCES

T. H. HUXLEY: Life and Letters of T. H. Huxley by his son, Leonard Huxley (Macmillan, 1900) Vol. 1, pp. 319, 337–351. 'Evolution and Ethics, The Romanes Lecture, 1893' (Macmillan 1893), pp. 36–37. 'On Descartes' Discourse on Method', Method and Results IV.

RENAN: From his revised Preface to *L'Avenir*.

CYRIL CONNOLLY: 'The Modern Movement: 100 Key Books from England, France and America, 1880–1950' (André Deutsch-Hamish Hamilton, 1965), pp. 6–9, 3, 85–86, 29, 31, 2, 5, 86.

BRIGID BROPHY: 'Fifty Works of English Literature Which We Could Do Without' by Brigid Brophy, Michael Levy and Charles Osborne (Rapp and Carroll, 1967), pp. 12, 96, 11, 36, 97, 31, 94, 81, 30, viii.

DR WILL DURANT: Article written for the Associated Press of America, as printed in *Long Island Press*, 22 December 1963.

PAMELA HANSFORD JOHNSON: 'On Iniquity' (Macmillan, 1967), pp. 129–30.

3
Permissive Storm-troopers

The apostles of total permissiveness have been described by Mr Kingsley Amis as those who buy unexamined the abortion-divorce-homosexuality-censor-
ship-marijuana package. 'Unexamined' and 'package'
are the key words in this description, for there are
obviously many thoughtful people who have serious
reasons for championing the legal reforms associated
with one or other of these words, and not everyone who
favours permissive legislation in one field thinks it
desirable in all the others.

Mr Malcolm Muggeridge believes that Britain is 'in
for a period when moral issues will loom larger than
any others – a state of affairs which will lead to some
interesting new alignments'. He wrote in the *New
Statesman* (11 August 1967):

> Taking my own case, as a strong opponent of the
> Abortion (Medical Termination of Pregnancy) Bill
> I found myself on the same side as Baroness Woot-
> ton, Wayland Young (Lord Kennet) and Mr Stevas;
> three people with whom I rarely agree. Again, as
> one who is violently opposed to any relaxation of
> control of so-called 'soft' drugs, I found myself en-
> thusiastically applauding a column by Lena Jeger
> in the *Guardian* which assembled some of the over-
> whelming evidence that cannabis is dangerous 'from
> every point of view, whether physical, mental, social
> or criminological'.

He attributes the Parliamentary preoccupation with moral questions to political causes:

> The fact is that, with Wilson a stronger Tory than most Tories, and Heath more Labour than Labour, there can't be any domestic political issues. . . . Governments in such a plight have to throw some sort of a bone to their discontented militants. The Tories, when they were in power, threw their militants commercial TV; Wilson has thrown his consenting adults and abortion – matters which raise moral issues cutting across accepted political and ideological categories.

This casts doubt on Mr Amis's over-simplified view that the drive to permissiveness is always the work of what he calls 'lefties' – a category in which he includes his recent self. For the champions of permissiveness are drawn from every party. Sir Edward Boyle, the Shadow Minister of Education, for example, wrote an enthusiastic final article in the *Guardian* series on The Permissive Society in October 1967. 'I do not myself believe that we are likely to see a general reaction against permissiveness,' he wrote, 'nor that we have any good reason to want this.' (*Guardian*, 20 October 1967).

Yet when all allowance has been made for the more thoughtful element and for the variation from country to country, it seems clear that the drive towards permissiveness in Western countries is spear-headed by the type of automatic permissive storm-trooper of whom Mr Amis writes. These people have endowed total permissiveness with the quality of infallible dogma, and are prone to get unusually excited when any restraint, either legal or self-imposed, is suggested.

Miss Pamela Hansford Johnson came up against this

attitude in her investigations into the Moors Murder Trial recorded in her book *On Iniquity*. In this trial, Ian Brady, aged 27, and Esther Myra Hyndley, aged 23, were convicted of murdering a girl of 10 and boys of 12 and 17 in particularly bestial cirumstances. The prosecution showed that the accused had soaked themselves in the literature of sadism and torture, including the works of the Marquis de Sade, and that these books had influenced them. The natural question, after such a case, was whether or not some measure of censorship might be desirable or whether, at least, authors and publishers should not practise some self-restraint lest they encourage the harming of other innocent children.

It was not surprising that publishers like Mr Maurice Girodias, who is on record that he is 'all for the corruption of youth', (*Sunday Times*, 28 February, 1965), should object violently to such a question being asked. But Miss Hansford Johnson found the reluctance to discuss this issue far more general:

The all-permissive, the 'swinging society': under its Big Top, the whole garish circus of the new freedom, freedom to revel, through all kinds of mass-media, in violence, in pornography, in sado-masochism. The walls of the police store-rooms are almost bulging outwards with the pressure of tons upon tons of dirty books – the ones still within the scope of the law. But there are plenty outside its scope, so we do not seem to be worrying about that just yet.

It is quite difficult, in England, to ask some simple question about the whole thing, such as 'Is what we are doing socially harmful?' 'Because of it, do some people get hurt?' and get a sober answer. Such a question not infrequently prompts unthinking tantrums, the tantrums of a child clutching to its breast some precious, grubby toy rabbit it cannot bear to part with.

And again:

There are very few intellectuals indeed who will now lend themselves to serious discussion as to whether, by mass communications of all kinds, we in the West are not poisoning that air, whether it may be due to its infection that some children die. In fact, any attempt to get them to discuss the subject responsibly and without exaggeration often drives them into a strange state of hysteria, of the curious kind of unreason one sometimes meets in religious controversy, or of total silence.

Miss Katharine Whitehorn, the *Observer* columnist, who states that she 'generally votes the straight progressive ticket', has noted something approaching this hysteria in the talk about divorce. 'I cannot help feeling it odd,' she wrote on 11 December 1966, 'that divorce is talked of in enlightened circles as if it were a benefit that should be available to all, rather than a tragedy it is worth almost anything to avoid.' She remarked that the Report of the Lord Chancellor's Law Commission spoke always of divorce as 'relief', 'as if the only possible picture of marriage were of two people gagged and bound together by the ties of Church and State'.

The danger is that words like divorce, abortion, censorship and the others employed in Mr Amis's description have become emotive words to which the permissive storm-trooper reacts with the predictability of Pavlov's conditioned dogs. A new orthodoxy has been created, a 'sleeping up with the Joneses ethos', to quote Miss Whitehorn again, which, in certain circles at least, 'puts the faithful and the virgin, if any, badly on the defensive'. 'In the age of freedom,' she writes, 'it is "that rarest of the sexual perversions, chastity" that is least readily allowed. At the present rate of going, chastity will have died out altogether in another fifty years.' (*The Observer*, 6 December 1965). Some seem to think this is an underestimate of the pace at which fashions are changing. The *Observer Colour Magazine* of 17 September 1967, devoted almost its entire issue to an enquiry entitled, 'Are We the Last Married Generation?'

The legislation which has floated through on this permissive tide has not always had happy results. The 1960 Gaming, Betting and Lotteries Act was, as Colin Bell pointed out in the *Weekend Telegraph* (30 September 1966), passed in an atmosphere of progressive euphoria:

One speaker in the debate referred to it as 'the clergyman's charter', apparently under the illusion that all it really did was permit lotteries to be run for good causes. One of its sponsors, Dennis Vosper, M.P. (now Lord Runcorn), went so far as to suggest 'that some of the lure and attraction of gambling will disappear when it becomes legal'.

Since the Act was supposed to be preventing any casinos at all, its failure can be measured by the fact that gaming-clubs in Britain now total up to 5,000, excluding Bingo clubs.

By passing the Act, Parliament rejected the moral arguments against the mere act of gambling. However, the arguments against it based on its social consequences have been steadily reinforced as each year has gone by.

By 1966, when the gambling turnover had risen to about a quarter of the national budget, the Home Office recognized that a mistake had been made, and the Parliamentary Secretary, Mr George Thomas, stated that 'unless a halt is called, we will be on the way to decadence from which it will be difficult to recover'. Subsequent legislation has not reversed the trend. Whether other permissive legislation – that, for example, on abortion – will have similar unforeseen results, it is too early to say. 'The way the Bill is working,' said Mr Richard Crossman, the responsible Minister, 'is giving grave alarm even to those who are keen supporters of the Bill.' (*The Times*, 15 April 1969.) In a House of Lords debate on one such measure, Lord Kilmuir remarked: 'Today we are rapidly drifting into the position that the obvious way of avoiding sin by not committing it is thought too difficult for mankind.'

One hopes that these new laws will bring relief to some individuals who find themselves, sometimes through no fault of their own, in distressing circumstances. But one is bound to note that the experience of other countries which have legalized abortion, for example, has not yet proved that we have discovered a simpler way of avoiding danger and unpleasantness than that advocated by Lord Kilmuir. In Jugoslavia, for instance, where a measure similar to that enacted in Britain has been law for some time, there appears to have been widespread damage to health. Comparing 1951 (before abortion was legalized) with 1959 (after it had been), cases of genital inflammation rose from 44,569 to 173,324, of menstrual disorders from 24,401 to 91,697, of sterility from 5,508 to 20,320, and of extra-uterine pregnancy from 489 to 1,167. The head of an abortion unit in a Swedish hospital, Dr E. Sjøvall, has stated that 'an abortion will always be a dangerous and unbiological method, since the sharp severance of all the processes in the body of a pregnant woman will often result in long lasting ill-health'. Such evidence can be multiplied, and emphasizes that if permissive legislation is taken as a signal for ever more permissive behaviour, the results can be disappointing.

Meanwhile London has become the abortion capital of Europe, and fortunes are being made by exploiting that fact.

Lord Clifford, after the passing of the Abortion Bill, wrote to *The Times* (27 October 1967):

> The real danger is in what is next to come from the same stable. Infanticide is now unnecessary. Euthanasia is probably first on the list: quite a popular subject with the theorists until one approaches that 'bourn from which no traveller returns': or maybe sterilization.
>
> Whichever it is we may be sure that our would-be reformers will continue to ignore the advice of those they order to do their dirty work for them – be it doctors, lawyers, or police.

Lord Longford, who, as Leader of the House of Lords, left the Front Bench to speak against the Abortion Bill, has similar fears. He was, he said, shocked by the proposals in this Bill, but far more so by what he thought lay behind them. He continued:

> Does anyone think that if this Bill goes through with acclamation and general congratulation the trend against the sanctity of human life will stop there? ... It is surely no accident ... that the President of the Abortion Law Reform Society, and their most formidable intellectual, should be that bril-

liant, dedicated, high-minded man Professor Glanville Williams, who recently deployed the argument for euthanasia in front of millions on television.

On that subject, he wrote in his most famous book . . . : 'At present the problem has certainly not reached the degree of seriousness that would warrant an effort being made to change the traditional attitudes towards the sanctity of life of the aged. Only the grimmest necessity could bring about a change' – that means, a change in the attitude towards the sanctity of the life of the aged – 'that . . . would probably cause apprehension and deep distress to many people and inflict a traumatic injury upon the accepted code of behaviour built up by 2,000 years of Christian religion. It may be, however, that as the problem becomes more acute it will itself cause a reversal of generally accepted values.' So the execution time of the old people may not be so very far off.

Lords Clifford and Longford have been proved right in their prophecies for, in March 1969, a Voluntary Euthanasia Bill was introduced in the House of Lords. *The Times* (24 March 1969) opposed it on several grounds, including what it called 'the slippery slope'. 'The progress of the law of abortion (where the legal grounds for destroying the foetus have expanded from the life of the mother, to the health of the mother, to the welfare of the children already born) confirms the suspicion that euthanasia once legally admitted would be similarly expanded.'

Mr Oliver Haskard suggested, in a letter to the paper (*The Times*, 29 March 1969) how easily this could happen. He wrote:

The following sequence is probable: —

1. I am old, I am terminally ill, I want to be killed.
2. I am old, I am terminally ill, I don't want to be a burden to my family and therefore I must ask to be killed.
3. I am terminally ill, or chronically sick (nobody quite knows). I would sooner stay alive for a bit, but it seems it would be selfish not to ask to be killed.
4. I am old, I am neither terminally ill nor chronically sick, but I am not much use to anybody and my children have to support me. I don't want to die but I suppose I should ask to be killed.
5. I am still quite young, but nobody loves me. I want to be killed.

Moral principles, Christian or otherwise, be damned. Sheer common sense must show the evil likely to result from this particular slippery slope.

Many advocates of these permissive bills were moved by a genuine compassion for individuals, though one wonders whether it is truly compassionate for churchmen at least to imply, by their silence, that there is no power whereby men can withstand temptation. Some of them have missed the distinctions drawn by Dr B. H. Streeter, the late Provost of the Queen's College, Oxford, when he wrote:

We do not view sheep-stealing as a virtue because we now think hanging was an excessive penalty; we may regard Parnell as hardly treated without approving of adultery. The tendency of certain types of conduct is to be socially and spiritually constructive, that of others is to be socially and spiritually disintegrating. It matters supremely to any society that it should have a clear principle for distinguishing between these two types, and that its average members should be able to say at once, this is on the side of right; that is on the side of wrong. It also matters, but it matters less, how many of its members fail, through the frailty of human nature, to live up to that principle. Granted in any society a clear knowledge of the right direction, then the steady pressure of the tone and example of the better elements – which always elicits an instinctive approval from the majority – will gradually lift the average standard of conduct.

REFERENCES

KINGSLEY AMIS: Article in *Sunday Telegraph*, 2 July 1967.

ABORTION: Results in Jugoslavia: Mojic A. Proc. 3rd International Conference on Planned Parenthood.
Dr E. Sjøvall: Report of 4th International Conference on Planned Parenthood. Quoted in *Sunday Times*, 13 February, 1966.

PAMELA HANSFORD JOHNSON: 'On Iniquity' (Macmillan, 1967), pp. 17, 33.

LORD LONGFORD: Hansard House of Lords Report for 19 July 1967, Vol. 285, No. 181, pp. 314–5.

B. H. STREETER: 'Adventure, The Faith of Science and the Science of Faith' (Macmillan, 1937), pp. 126–7.

4
The Pro-Pot Lobby

'It was a surprise, if not a shock, for many people to learn
from the notorious advertisement in *The Times* that there
was a pro-pot lobby in this country. . . . My mind boggles at
the thought of licensing the local tobacconist or off-licence
to sell cannabis, thus creating centres where people could
start on one drug and then easily move to another.'

> The Rt. Hon. James Callaghan,
> Home Secretary, in the House of
> Commons, 27 January 1969.

'If people think they're going to get any fulfilment in Art
through taking drugs, then they're in for a hell of a dis-
appointment. Because on tape recordings of people under
LSD it's been shown they speak absolute drivel. Taking
drugs as a short cut to God is absolute drivel as. well.'

> W. H. Auden
> (*Sunday Telegraph*, 29 October, 1967)

A major effort of the permissive lobby through the
world is now concentrated on the legalization of
marijuana, otherwise known as cannabis or pot, one
of the milder of the hallucinogens. As this drug was
banned in almost every country under the International Convention on Narcotic Drugs in 1961, it is
recognized that the legal dikes are formidable, but
marijuana enthusiasts have high hopes that the permissive tide in Britain may be strong enough to
breach them. Hence the formation of SOMA – the
Society of Mental Awareness – and the mounting
campaign in Britain.

As marijuana and other drugs are often presented
as 'a short-cut to God' or even as a substitute religion,

anyone wishing to mount a Christian counter-attack must take note of this campaign.

The British public first became aware of this organized campaign when the London Flower Children demonstrated in Hyde Park during the visit of Mr Allen Ginsberg, who describes himself as 'an aging sex-fiend, dope-fiend, communalist, anarchist, visionary and scribe'. (*The Times*, 13 July, 1967). This was followed on July 24 by SOMA's full page advertisement in *The Times* headed 'The law against marijuana is immoral in principle and unworkable in practice'.

The list of signatories reads like a roll of the permissive élite, with the addition of Mr Brian Epstein (who tragically died of an overdose of barbiturates soon afterwards), three Beatles, two Nobel Prize Winners (but not in medicine), Tariq Ali, and two psychiatrists, Dr David Stafford-Clark and Dr Anthony Storr. But a letter to *The Times* (28 July 1967) pointed out, 'the list of signatories does not include any doctor who has made any intensive study of cannabis, and perhaps the most significant feature of it is the names which do not appear'.

This advertisement merits detailed study because, in spite of all that has happened since, it remains the classic statement of the arguments for legalizing cannabis. The Wootton Committee Report, which recommended the reduction of legal penalties, came out against legalization, and found it significant that 'even those who saw least danger in the drug wanted to discourage juveniles from using it'. Some of the Committee's *obiter dicta*, like its recommendations, were considered by the Home Secretary to be 'overinfluenced' by the writers of 'the notorious advertisement in *The Times*', a charge which Lady Wootton denied but which re-emphasized the importance of that advertisement.

The text of the advertisement began by stating that the 'use of cannabis is increasing', especially among 'writers, teachers, doctors, musicians, etc.' It then stated that 'smoking the herb is a traditional part of social life for hundreds of thousands of immigrants'. Neither point seems conclusive.

A leading article in *The Lancet* of 9 November, 1963, was then quoted as declaring that 'it is worth considering . . . giving cannabis the same legal status as alcohol', but the further fact that *The Lancet*'s editorial gave strong reasons against legalization is not mentioned. Nor is it anywhere stated that Britain is bound by an international treaty, signed by some sixty countries, not to legalize the drug.

The advertisement also stated that the present law discourages necessary research into the drug. Upon this, Professor F. E. Camps of the Department of Forensic Medicine at the London Hospital Medical College wrote to us: 'There is no hampering of research by law if it is *genuine* and hence supplies of the drug are obtainable from official sources.'

Much was made of the difficulties which the police have in enforcing the law and of their alleged brutality in doing so. The first point is invalid, for the police also have difficulty in enforcing the law against stealing. The second point is greatly exaggerated. Police are mainly concerned with convicting 'pushers'. Indeed, Professor Camps stated that the police would 'very nearly have control of the problem, if it were not for these "great" people (the advertisement's signatories) saying this and that'. (*Daily Express*, 30 October, 1967.)

The crux of the argument for legalizing marijuana is that the drug is 'harmless, non-addictive and does not lead on to heroin addiction'. The writers of *The Times* advertisement here stated:

The main justification for the prohibition of cannabis has been the contention that its use leads to
heroin addiction. This contention does not seem
to be supported by any documented evidence, and
has been specifically refuted by several authoritative
studies. It is almost certainly correct to state that
the risk to cannabis smokers of becoming heroin
addicts is far less than the risk to drinkers of becoming alcoholics.

Cannabis is usually taken by normal persons for
the purpose of enhancing sensory experience.
Heroin is taken almost exclusively by weak and
disturbed individuals for the purpose of withdraw-
ing from reality. By prohibiting cannabis Parliament has created a black market where heroin
could occasionally be offered to persons who would
not otherwise have had access to it. Potential addicts,
having found cannabis to be a poor escape route,
have doubtless been tempted to try heroin; and it
is probable that their experience of the harmless-
ness and non-addictive quality of cannabis has led
them to underestimate the dangers of heroin. It is
the prohibition of cannabis, and not cannabis itself,
which may contribute to heroin addiction.

In support of this argument, medical opinions were
quoted, notably those of the medical signatories,
Dr Stafford-Clark and Dr Storr, which we reprint here
in full. Dr Stafford-Clark, who is Director of Psychological Medicine at Guy's Hospital – whose *Gazette* was
also quoted – wrote:

Certain specific myths require objective confronta-
tion since otherwise they recurrently confuse the
issue, and incidentally divert the energy and attention of police and customs and immigration authori-

ties in directions which have very little to do with facts and much more to do with prejudiced beliefs. The relative innocence of marijuana by comparison with alcohol is one such fact, its social denial a comparable myth.

Dr Storr was quoted as saying:

Marijuana is not a drug of addiction and is, medically speaking, far less harmful than alcohol or tobacco. It is generally smoked in the company of others and its chief effect seems to be an enhanced appreciation of music and colour together with a feeling of relaxation and peace. A mystical experience of being at one with the universe is common, which is why the drug has been highly valued in Eastern religions. Unlike alcohol, marijuana does not lead to aggressive behaviour, nor is it aphrodisiac. There is no hangover, nor, so far as it is known, any deleterious physical effect.

Both in the main text and in these supporting opinions, much weight was laid upon marijuana being less harmful than alcohol. 'But,' asked Dr Salvino Caruana, the Deputy Medical Director of the Central Council for Medical Education, 'because we have accepted alcohol and are prepared to put up with it, is this a valid argument for accepting another factor – a more dangerous, more crippling, more hopeless one – in our midst?' (*Daily Express*, 31 July, 1967). Dr Caruana thinks marijuana more dangerous than alcohol because 'whereas those who drink alcohol become confused and know they are confused, the person who smokes marijuana is also confused, but does not know it. This makes him a danger to himself and to others.' He adds: 'The idea of a few hundred thousand hard drug addicts in our midst should kill immediately any desire or temptation we might develop of legalizing drug-taking for kicks.'

SOMA's claim, in *The Times* advertisement, that marijuana itself is harmless did not go unchallenged. Dr J. A. Harrington, Consulting Psychiatrist and the Medical Director at the Uffculme Clinic, Birmingham – a clinic 'much involved in the problem of drug addiction' – was one of a dozen doctors whose letters were printed in *The Times*. He wrote on 27 July, 1967:

The medical opinions quoted by SOMA (24 July) are one-sided and require rebuttal.

Marijuana is taken mainly for its pleasant intoxicating effects and like all intoxicants, its relationship to accidents of all types cannot be ignored. Its effects on mental state, though transient, are profound. Euphoria and escape from the realities of everyday problems easily makes its use become a habit, which is not harmless to the young. It often inhibits higher mental control and releases repressed desires and fantasies. Its significance as a stimulus in persons already prone to crime and violence, therefore, should not be discounted lightly.

Admittedly the immature, the weak and inadequate, and the frankly psychopathic, are most likely to fall victims to its charms, but the fact that it is harmless when properly used is no reason for any medical endorsement of its widespread use. To suggest that research will solve the problem no more than begs the question. As with the attitudes to alcohol, the issue is clouded by emotional biases which will not be changed by further scientific investigation. It is not the drug but the person who uses it.

Dr Felix Brown, physician in charge of psychological medicine at the Royal Free Hospital, added that the attraction of marijuana lay not in its being illicit, but in the fact that it 'induces a withdrawn, euphoric, dreamy, hallucinatory state'. 'I have not seen a regular hashish smoker in whom this habit has not become, if not the main, one of the main experiences of his life. Love, career, ambition, home and family formation seem to take a second place. It seems to hit at the very motivation of human life.' (*The Times*, 29 July 1967.)

The advocates of legalizing cannabis consider such statements irrelevant because that drug does not lead on to heroin. What are the facts?

Miss Alice Bacon, the then Minister of State at the Home Office, said in the House of Commons on 28 July, 1967, that '97 per cent of heroin addicts known to the Home Office started drug-taking by using cannabis'. The Recorder of Birmingham, Mr Malcolm Argyle, Q.C., declared that out of 70 registered heroin addicts in Birmingham, 69 had begun on cannabis. (*The Times*, 28 July 1967.) 'In this city,' he said, 'the question of cannabis is not an intellectual or academic exercise, but a practical problem. In this court I have seen again and again kids – one cannot describe them as anything other than children – from good homes and with good work records suddenly literally change their preferences in every way, finishing up as what can only be described as human wrecks.'

The legalizers say that these figures prove nothing. They say that all heroin addicts drink tea and coffee, and no one dreams of saying that they have progressed from these beverages.

Professor W. D. M. Paton, Professor of Pharmacology at Oxford, in his lecture at the Dundee Meeting of the British Association on 26 August 1968, pointed out that this argument 'ignores the crucial point that coffee and tea drinking is an extremely common activity, but cannabis-taking a much less common one in the general population'. 'It is in the comparison between normal incidence and the incidence among addicts that the significance arises,' he adds. 'This sort of argument is of the same kind as that which associates cancer of the lung with smoking, silicosis with certain dusts, industrial use of β-napthylamine with bladder cancer, damage to blood-forming organs with chloramphenicol, consumption of alcohol with traffic accidents, and the like.' The Professor analyses the figures in detail and comes to the conclusion that there is a 'far closer connection between cannabis and the opiates than is generally recognized'. We have reprinted his Table, which supports the conclusion of Miss Bacon and the Recorder of Birmingham, at the end of this chapter.

Experts incline to agree that there is no biological effect from using marijuana which primes users for the hard drugs, and it is still happily true that the majority of marijuana-smokers do not go on to heroin. But the Home Office figures show that those who join the drug cult through marijuana are far more likely to proceed to heroin than those who never join it. And the likelihood of proceeding to LSD, or some other so-called 'soft' drug is still higher – for, in many circles, they are interchangeable. 'Addicts,' states Professor Paton, 'infect other addicts.'

LSD, though not, like heroin, a killer, is already proving to have most disturbing qualities. *The Observer* of 2 April, 1967, reported from New York:

Adults who take the mind-expanding drug LSD may be threatening the physical and mental health of future generations. This is the view of two American scientists who have spent the past years studying the effects of the drug upon human tissue and cells. Their research, which is probably the first of its kind, has led Dr Nathan Back and Dr Maimon M. Cohen to believe that LSD can cause damage to the human chromosomes – tiny carriers of heredity contained in every human cell . . .

Commenting on the results, Dr Back said: 'Our initial studies have led us to the conclusion that LSD can cause changes in the chromosomes similar to certain types of hereditary diseases like Bloom's Syndrome and Sanconi's Anaemia.'

The Saturday Evening Post of August, 1967, gives details of such research in several parts of the United States. The introduction to the article reads:

In Oregon, a young mother brought her newborn baby in to be examined. The child had a defect of the intestinal tract and its head was developing grotesquely – one side growing at a much faster rate than the other.

A mental patient in New York and six young men in Oregon were found to have extensive damage of their heritage carrying chromosomes – damage of the type that is known to result in misshapen and defective babies.

Two of the young men in Oregon also were found to have a chromosomal abnormality that seems to be identical with the first stages of leukemia, the incurable blood cancer that proliferated at Hiroshima after the bomb fell.

A graduate student in Los Angeles has twice

undergone typical epileptic *grand mal* convulsions – one time with seizures so violent that he broke two vertebrae.

The young mother, the mental patient in New York, the young men in Oregon and the graduate student – along with several thousands of new mental-hospital inmates – all have one thing in common. They all took LSD.

The *British Medical Journal* commented editorially on American research that more work is needed to assess the potential danger, and adds:

At this stage, however, it can be stated with certainty that LSD, as well as being a potential risk to the mind of the user, may also cause chromosomal abnormalities, foetal malformations, and possibly leukemia.

In *The New Morality*, we stated that we were less concerned with the increase of sexual immorality among the young than with the increase of intellectual immorality among the middle-aged. So with drugs, and the permissive society generally, it is the intellectual who condones indulgence rather than the teenager who gives way to temptation whom we decry. We agree with Mr Quintin Hogg when he said at Brighton:

I do not know if you saw the signatories to *The Times* advertisement (on marijuana). There was an old Lancing boy among them. . . .

This conference opened with four Lancing boys expelled, their early careers of promise gravely damaged, if not ruined: But who are we to blame? Who are the old to blame the young? Is it these kids of 15 or 16 who have suffered enough for their folly but, I hope, will learn how to repair it?

Or is it those sometime members of their old school who publish advertisements in the press on subjects of which they can know nothing with a moral blindness and perversity which disgraces the name of a Christian country? (*The Times*, 21 October 1967.)

NOTE

The association between cannabis and heroin:
Professor Paton in his lecture to the British Association which as printed in *Advancement of Science*, December 1968, pp. 200–212, wrote:

> It is over the last two to three years that the idea that cannabis might 'escalate' to heroin has been canvassed really seriously in this country; and one can find some quite wise authorities who have said that they see no evidence for it. I have reached a different conclusion. But first one must be clear what one is saying: not that every person who takes cannabis is bound to go on to heroin; nor that I can identify *a priori* a process, started by cannabis, which must, physiologically or chemically, go on to heroin. It is simply a question of public health statistics: is there evidence or is there not, that taking cannabis gives an enhanced risk of addiction to opiates, and if so, by how much. If there *is* such enhancement, then the social cost of cannabis includes not only its own dangers, but that of the 'harder' drugs to which it may lead. . . .
>
> Apart from knowing that cannabis is particularly associated with heroin, one would like to get an estimate of something for which an incidence is very difficult to get by direct enquiry, i.e. the incidence of heroin-taking among cannabis-takers. This one can do by using a method of inverse probability (a version of Bayes' theorem), used, *inter alia*, by astronomers, for whom comparable difficulties exist in making *direct* experiments on their objects of study. This calculation gives an incidence of 7 to 15 per cent, i.e. that of those who take cannabis, 7 to 15 in every 100 will be, or are, heroin-takers (Table 1). The only other definite figure I have seen published is that by Dr Elisabeth Tylden, from a study of a group of 130 hashish smokers, of whom 10 per cent were known to be taking morphine and/or heroin.

I think one is bound to conclude that there is, at least for our culture, a far closer connection between cannabis and the opiates than is generally recognized.

TABLE 1

ASSOCIATION OF HEROIN WITH OTHER DRUGS

Drug X	Incidence of X-taking generally	Incidence of X-taking among heroin-takers	Estimated probability of heroin-taking among X-takers
Coffee or tea	100 per cent	100 per cent	5 per 100,000
Alcohol	70	33	2 to 3 per 100,000 1500 per 100,000
Amphetamine (non-medical)	0·2	57	(1·5 per cent)
Cannabis	0·03 to 0·06 % (30 to 60 per 100,000)	88	7000-15,000 per 100,000 (7-15 per cent)

Overall incidence of heroin-taking: approximately 5 per 100,000 of population.

Probability of A (given B) =
      Probability of A ×
Probability of B (given A)
      Probability of B

where A = heroin-taking and B = taking drug X. (Data from Chapple, 1966, Bewley, 1966, and Kessel and Walton, 1967).

5
The 'Affectless Society'?

'You cannot play with the animal in you without becoming wholly animal, play with falsehood without forfeiting your right to truth, play with cruelty without losing your sensitivity of mind. He who wants to keep his garden tidy doesn't reserve a plot for weeds.'

DAG HAMMARSKJÖLD

'Not having found a major cause, they proceed to great emotional energy in minor ones, and of the minor ones, verbal emancipation has taken a high place. . . . With the same amount of passion spent on social purposes, America might now have a Health Service and Britain might be able to earn a living.'

PAMELA HANSFORD JOHNSON

During her investigation into the Moors Murders, to which we referred in Chapter 3, Miss Hansford Johnson concluded that 'we are in danger of creating an Affectless Society, in which nobody cares for anyone but himself, or for anything but instant self-gratification. 'We demand sex without love, violence for "kicks",' she writes. 'We are encouraging the blunting of sensibility: and this, let it be said, was not the way to an Earthly Paradise, but the way to Auschwitz.'

This may, at first sight, seem an odd conclusion to reach about an age which has produced the Welfare State in Scandinavia, the British Health Service, the American Great Society and other attempts at greater social justice, and which is busy everywhere softening up the social laws based on a 'puritanical' Christian morality. Yet people are less certain today than ten years ago that the Welfare State of itself has made us more thoughtful of our neighbours; and it has seldom been those classes and peoples which allowed themselves the greatest measure of self-indulgence which have been most sensitive to the lot of the less fortunate. Rome before Christianity was both profligate and brutal, and the British aristocracy of the Enlightenment, whose highly cultured life was built on child labour and the slave trade, displayed a similar combination of qualities. 'The venality of English political life in the eighteenth century,' writes John Marlowe, 'was the counterpart of the coarseness and profligacy of the social life of the English governing class. And there was a quality about it more repellent than venality – the quality of heartlessness.' It took the emergence of more exacting Christian standards as practised by men like Wilberforce and Shaftesbury to reverse the trends to profligacy and heartlessness and to initiate the needed reforms.

An extreme example of the Affectless Society appears in the transcript of the Moors trial itself. David Smith, the unwilling accomplice of the child murderers, Brady and Hyndley, describing Brady at work on one of his victims, said: 'I have seen butchers working in the shops show as much emotion as he did when they are cutting up a sheep's ribs.'

The Attorney-General asked Brady, in this connection: 'What were your feelings when striking the boy with this axe? What were your emotions?'

Brady replied, 'I didn't have any. I can't remember what my emotions were. I was just hitting him.'

Less obvious examples of the same callousness appear more and more in our social life. Mr John Updike, in his best-selling novel, *The Couples*, describes life in a small New England town called Tarbox, where primitive American democracy still reveals itself in town meetings and three streets in the business district are named Hope, Charity and Divinity. 'The couples,' writes *Time* Magazine's reviewer (26 April 1968), 'have made sex by turns their toy, their glue, their trauma, their therapy, their hope, their frustration, their revenge, their narcotic, their main line of communication and their sole and pitiable shield against the awareness of death. Adultery, says Updike, has become a kind of "imaginative quest" for a successful hedonism that would enable man to enjoy an otherwise meaningless life. But to seek pleasure is not necessarily to find it. The couples of Tarbox live in a place and time that together seem to have been ordained for the quest. "Welcome," says Georgene Thorne, "to the postpill paradise." Leisure, cars and babysitters give them mobility to track any pleasure. "All these goings on would be purely lyrical like nymphs and satyrs," said Updike recently, "except for the group of distressed and neglected children."'

The progress of events in Britain was documented in the *Observer Colour Magazine* enquiry, 'Are We the Last Married Generation?' 'Now, for the first time,' wrote the editors in their introduction, 'marriage itself is being eyed for its possible unsuitability to human nature'. 'Marriage will have to disintegrate. It's too demanding and crippling,' wrote one of the contributors. 'And children are really self-sufficient at 14. . . .'

Commenting on the survey as a whole in *The Observer* of 1 October 1967, Katharine Whitehorn wrote:

At least the whole social framework (in Victorian times) did ensure that once you had taken the plunge and got married you were stuck with it: as you made your bed so did you lie on it – or at worst had a bed made up in the dressing-room. Nobody said, 'There, there, dear, it was just a boyish mistake' and got you out of it; nobody thought that if you shut your eyes and took a deep breath your wife and children would simply disappear like spots before the eyes. Yet that is often what I feel the softies of the modern age expect. . . . They are liberal enough to sympathize, when talking about a distressed friend or criminal, with the problems of children of broken homes – and then go right ahead and organize a broken home for their own . . .

. . . I would like, just once, to hear someone say of a man who has left his wife and four fat babies right in the middle of the kitchen floor, *not* that he's been through a hard time lately, or that his mother was a very complicated woman, or that he's worried about his job, or that he married very young; but simply, 'You louse.'

Another example of how this Affectless Society, with its addiction to violence springs from extreme permissiveness, is seen in the United States of America. On 2 May 1968, Mr Ian Brodie reported from New York:

The land of Mom and apple pie, of the Bible belt and the Hollywood code of decency, is developing – or deteriorating – from a rather Puritan society into a totally permissive one. And the candidates in the presidential election are being hit hard by it.

The keys to this personality change are a number of Supreme Court decisions which virtually outlaw censorship and decree that obscenity is not illegal.

The ugliest side effect is the stream of venom released in print against the country's established leadership. . . .

The unsubtle technique is simply to represent the President, Senator Kennedy and others as sexually perverted monsters . . . .

'If it goes on,' one Washington expert said, 'it will drive many people out of public life . . . .'

'It is a curious irony that the Supreme Court, dedicated to preserving the freedom which is the foundation of American life, has confused it with licence. In doing so it has given its seal of approval to the sick society which will undermine the United States from within.' (*Daily Express*, 2 May, 1968.)

When, just five weeks later, Senator Robert Kennedy had been shot, David English, the foreign editor of the *Daily Express,* commented:

If there is total licence to commit character assassination is it surprising that the real thing becomes a conditioned reflex of the times?

The freedom to poison the mind with hatred and fear, to publish filth and lies about the men who wish to take on the onerous task of leading the country has become blindly accepted in the United States . . . .

Last month in America, I read articles about Robert Kennedy's life and family motivated by a malice and hatred so pathological that no civilized printer should have handled them. But there they were. On the bookstalls. And when I asked how it could happen . . . I was told 'We have the freest Press in the world.' (*Daily Express*, 6 June 1968.)

Time (14 June, 1968), in its essay 'Politics and

Assassination', came to much the same conclusion:

> Equally inflammatory to unstable minds is the
> rising hyperbole of U.S. political debate. Race,
> Vietnam, crime – all lend themselves to verbal
> overkill, not so much by candidates as by extremists:
> the John Birchers, the Rap Browns, the most ardent
> war critics, the Klu Kluxers. The evidence is
> everywhere. In Dallas, Assistant District Attorney
> William Alexander snarls on a TV show: 'Earl
> Warren shouldn't be impeached – he should be
> hanged.' Cries Rap Brown, 'How many whites did
> you kill today?' Lyndon Johnson is routinely
> excoriated as a mass murderer. Robert Kennedy
> was branded by some San Francisco hippies as a
> 'fascist pig'. Eventually verbal assassination becomes
> physical assassination.

Here, as so often, extreme permissiveness leads to
extreme censorship for as Bernard Shaw once wrote,
'Assassination is the extreme form of censorship.'

Mr James Reston, the columnist and editorial
director of the *New York Times,* writing in the hours
when the Senator hung between life and death, put
it more broadly:

> Robert Kennedy is only the latest victim of a modern
> world that has turned loose greater forces than it
> can control. The struggles between the nations,
> between the races, between the rich and poor, be-
> tween the individual and bewildering change have
> produced a plague of lawlessness and violence that
> is now sweeping the globe.
> The pressures of all this are too much for weak
> and demented minds. The assassins of President
> John Kennedy, the Rev. Dr Martin Luther King,

and Lee Harvey Oswald, and the attacker of Senator
Kennedy may merely be deranged demons, tor-
mented by frustrations and intoxicated by fear or
revenge. But there is something more to it than
that.

This is not merely rejection of the view that life
is essentially decent, rational and peaceful, or even
a decline into individual moral insanity. There is
something in the air of the modern world: a
defiance of authority, a contagious irresponsibility,
a kind of moral delinquency, no longer restrained
by religious or ethical faith.

Mr Reston was right to emphasize that the problem
is world wide. For as Mr Jay Williams pointed out
in *The Times* (10 June 1968), 'that air of violence
is by no means an American prerogative: to say so
is to ignore everything that has happened in the
world since the rise of Hitler and Stalin.' Europe
has, during the years when Mr Connolly's Modern
Movement was at its height, generated more violence
than at any time in its history, and the end is not yet.

Many who are too young to remember Hitler or
even Stalin now believe that violence is the only way
to get results. They are to be found on both sides
of the race conflict in America and Africa, and among
an increasing number of students in every continent.
Advocates of student power maintain that it is not
they, but society, which is violent, and that they are
merely defending themselves; but in view of the forc-
ible occupation of universities and the training in
street warfare which some of them have undergone,
this would seem to be a theoretical rather than a
practical distinction. 'There is no cant from Cohn-
Bendit about violence being the last resort,' Brian
Waldron writes in his review of Cohn-Bendit's

Obsolete Communism. 'On the contrary, he likes street battles and considers that it is the duty and pleasure of a revolutionary to engineer them.' (*The Observer*, 24 November, 1968.)

This is not to say that the authorities or the *status quo* advocates are guiltless. Negroes are driven to extremes by white society's refusal to reform, and students have been sickened by the complacency and materialism of their elders. Violence begets violence. Mr Quintin Hogg, commenting on television about events of May 1968 in Paris, spoke of 'the things which begin to happen to people and to nations who lose faith in the ballot box,' and added, 'Both sides degenerate, both become brutal.' (*The Times*, 28 May 1968.)

Some psychologists comfort themselves by asserting that world war is no longer likely and that the violence within society is a less harmful substitute – or is even a 'ritual battle' like that carried on between animals.

Martin Luther King did not take that line. He contended that violence was less appropriate for the American Negro than for a people fighting against a foreign invader, precisely because the battle was within the nation.

The American Negro is not in a Congo where the Belgians will go back to Belgium after the battle is over, or in an India where the British will go back to England after independence is won. In the struggle for national independence one can talk about liberation now and integration later, but in the struggle for racial justice in a multi-racial society where the oppressor and the oppressed are both 'at home', liberation must come through integration.

He added:

> Are we seeking power for power's sake? Or are we
> seeking to make the world and our nation better
> places to live? If we seek the latter, violence can
> never provide the answer. The ultimate weakness
> of violence is that it is a descending spiral, be-
> getting the very thing it seeks to destroy. Instead
> of diminishing evil, it multiplies it. Through
> violence you may murder the liar, but you cannot
> murder the lie, nor establish the truth. Through
> violence you may murder the hater, but you do
> not murder hate. In fact, violence merely increases
> hate. So it goes. Returning violence for violence
> multiplies violence, adding deeper darkness to a
> night already devoid of stars. Darkness cannot drive
> out darkness: only light can do that. Hate cannot
> drive out hate: only love can do that.

The growth of violence in the modern world has
led many psychologists and sociologists to study the
roots of aggression. Many of them are coming to agree
with Jung that it is a human instinct as fundamental
as sex. Like sex, it can be used for good or for ill.
If misused, it brings damage to others and chaos to
society; but if used constructively it is the force which
enables men to initiate, to create, to master situations
and overcome difficulties.

This brings man back to the old basic choice. Will
he do good or evil? Will he use his powers constructively or destructively? And in this connection some
words of *The Observer* editorial on 27 October 1968,
the day of the demonstration in Grosvenor Square,
are worth pondering. 'What is still revolutionary in
human experience,' this editorial concluded, 'is a
society in which legal force is used only to protect

the individual's right to peaceful self-expression – a right which can be won and maintained only by controlling man's endemic tendency to resort to force. If today there are clashes between violent demonstrators and policemen who try to remain non-violent, it is undoubtedly the police who will be representing the really revolutionary principle.'

REFERENCES

PAMELA HANSFORD JOHNSON: 'On Iniquity' (Macmillan, 1967), pp. 84–5, 18, 35.

JOHN MARLOWE: 'The Puritan Tradition in English Life' (Cresset, 1957), p. 66.

MARTIN LUTHER KING: 'Chaos or Community' (Hodder & Stoughton, 1968), pp. 62–3.

6

Student Violence

Of all the forms of violence now prevalent in the Western world, that which puzzles the average person most is student violence. People of the older generation who either could not afford a university education, or obtained one as a result of parental sacrifice, find it hard to understand why young people who are being educated at the taxpayer's expense should want to paralyse their universities or spend their time plotting revolution. Young workers, too, who are taxpayers not grant receivers are no less impatient. The danger of a backlash exists in many parts of the world.

Student violence has, of course, been a familiar feature in some countries for decades. The potential of organized youth has long been realized by political parties of left and right in Asian countries, and their intervention has often been effective in Japan, Indonesia and in South America. It was first introduced into the Western world at Berkeley, California, and from there spread East to Columbia University, New York, Berlin, Paris and the London School of Economics.

In many of these places genuine and widespread student grievances existed – or still exist. These range from overcrowding to inadequate student grants, from non-communication between staff and students to anomalies about student discipline, and it is probable that, if such general grievances had not been allowed to fester, student extremists would have found it hard to mobilize so many students for their demonstrations. Also, here as elsewhere, plan beats no plan, and the apathy of the majority has often left extremists able to manipulate the masses – or pack the committees. For even though they are, in most countries, divided into mutually suspicious groups, the extremists are broadly united in their war against the 'system' and have the dynamism to carry others with them. They are also adept at choosing issues where university or national authorities can be provoked into violence or seeming injustice, issues on which they can gain more general support.

What are the extremist students after? Trevor Fisk, then President of the National Union of Students in Britain, writes in the Young Fabian Pamphlet, *Students Today*:

> They are Utopian in the sense of one recent press description of their stimulus: 'One of the basic motivations of the adherents of student power is hostility towards contemporary technological society.' Not to the evils of that society, a reformist position, but to that society as such. They are romantic in their identification of themselves as the new student class, a view easily, though somewhat mistakenly, confirmed by reading Herbert Marcuse. Students are a special political class because they are 'the only adults not absorbed into the productive sphere'. They alone can form 'that enlightened élite' which can define 'truth and falsehood' and decide for society *'who is to be tolerated'*. They have the same right then to dictate to society as Hitler's master race and Marx's vanguard of the proletariat. The acceptance by any

student of such totalistic dogma would be pathetic if it were not also dangerous.

In the same pamphlet, Peter Scott, who is described as 'a reporter on *The Times Literary Supplement*', states:

Perhaps the key word of any description of radical students is alienation. Partly this is a genuine feeling that our present society is depressingly materialistic and unjust, that conventionality and mediocrity and hypocrisy are hidden under the cloak of free speech and freedom; partly this is a pose. It is very doubtful how many people in Britain today can wholeheartedly desire a revolution and the inevitable human suffering that this would involve; probably students, however addicted to revolution as a theoretical concept, are not among them. Beneath the determinist language and the Marxist phrases the student revolutionary is sometimes a romantic at heart. It is not revolution with all its hardship that is their true goal; what they seek is the alienation of the revolutionary who has rejected society and its hypocrisy.

Mr Scott adds that the reason why so small a minority can lead others is that many more feel alienated from the world of their parents.

Neal Ascherson, in his perceptive article in *The Observer* (2 June 1968) summarized the extremists' philosophy as succinctly as anyone. After remarking on the influence of such varied personalities as Che Guevara and Mao, Herbert Marcuse and Wilhelm Reich, he wrote:

The professor and the guerrilla, the chairman and

the psychologist, are illustrations to a revolutionary text which – allowing for different traditions – reads much the same wherever the young go on the street. Parliaments are moribund; liberalism is a dangerous sham concealing the most efficient repression ever known. Moscow and Washington are power bureaucracies, brainwashing their masses by a manipulated Press into believing they are content. Society should be run by spontaneous workers' councils, by continuous democracy. Capitalism leads these days towards a sort of technocratic Fascism (and French and German students believe that Mr Wilson demonstrates this): it must go. Then a new human being will arise: unexploited, creative in the leisure granted by automation, spontaneous, uninhibited, social. And, if the truth be told, it is this New Adam who is the only hero the students really worship.

The 'new Adam' which they seek, like the new society which they believe will somehow spontaneously emerge out of the chaos of destruction, is inextricably bound up with a 'new' attitude to sex. Thus Mr Ascherson remarked:

Everywhere the works of Wilhelm Reich turn up: his fantastic synthesis of Freud and revolutionary politics, his account of the politically explosive nature of sexual relationships, his hypnotic diagrams showing sexual starvation leading to revolution, are squirted in paint on the Sorbonne walls or chucked at policemen's heads (in soft covers) by the free-living Communes of Berlin.

Dr George Steiner of Churchill College, Cambridge, considers this to be a crucial element. The removal, for the first time in history, of the fear of venereal disease and of unwanted pregnancies has meant that when young people make love, they are 'for the first time accountable to none but themselves; their act provides no hold for society, it need give no hostages.' (*The Sunday Times*, 21 July, 1968.) 'I believe,' he adds, 'that this liberation at the core has released enormous psychic energies. . . . When the student radicals of Berkeley, Nanterre or Amsterdam tell us that Reich's *Function of the Orgasm* is one of the sources of their politics, they are telling the truth. And we had better listen.'

Dr Steiner finds the dominant voices in the student revolt to be not Marcuse or Guevara, but the ancestral voices of Jarry, of Sade and Lautremont. 'But,' he adds, 'the name that comes up most often is that of Artaud, the contriver of the "theatre of cruelty". A psychologically infirm but intensely talented man, Artaud walked, and indeed mapped, the entire *via dolorosa* of the modern extremists: "happenings", drugs, insanity, suicide. . . . Behind the most radical elements in the student movement lies the fantasti-cations, the lyric anarchy, the Dada gestures and search for hallucinations which mark symbolist litera-ture and the art and drama of the 1920s and 1930s.' If this is so, M. Malraux, the French Minister of Culture, has no right to be surprised when violence and counter-violence break out in Paris streets for, as we have seen, it was he who unveiled the statue of the founder of Dada, who thought de Sade 'the freest spirit who ever lived'.

The danger of this violence and counter-violence were analysed in *The Times* editorial of 5 October 1968 entitled 'The British Backlash'. 'In Britain and perhaps in the whole world,' it states, 'the revolt of students is producing a contrary resentment which could prove more formidable than anything the students can do . . . The danger of anarchy is likely, even in this country, to lead to a more authoritarian social life.'

This editorial examines the connection between permissiveness and violence. After stating that Britain's greater permissiveness 'must have meant that some people made great mistakes in their lives, but for others the change has widened opportunities and made for a happier life', it continued:

The permissive society is one thing; its obvious fault, of which the flower children were an instance, is its softness and weakness. The violent society is something different again, and it is the violence of society against which people are reacting in America and here. Hobbesian Conservatives will find it natural that the permissive society and the violent society should go hand in hand. Certainly there are significant connections between the two. During the period when discipline has been steadily relaxed, violent crime has steadily risen. The advocates of complete freedom of sexual exhibition on the stage and in the cinema have also been the heralds of the theatre of cruelty. There is no doubt in human nature a connection between the self-indulgence of a spoilt child and the cruelty of a spoilt child.

Hobbesian Conservatives are not alone in seeing a connection between permissiveness and student violence. It was a writer in *The Black Dwarf* who declared that Marcuse was unduly suspicious of 'sexual freedom' and Mr Perry Anderson, the editor of the *New Left*, in his television discussion with Mr Quintin Hogg and Mr George Woodcock went out of his way to establish the link. When Mr Hogg and Mr Woodcock said they did not think that the violence of Paris was likely to be repeated in Britain, Mr Anderson replied:

> Some years ago Britain was known for repression, puritanism and hypocrisy, but British youth now lead in moral, sexual and aesthetic emancipation. I see no reason why British youth should not be in the vanguard of political emancipation as well.'

But it is not only the prophets of the 'modern movement' who have created this permissive, potentially violent youth. Sociologists and psychologists in America, according to Richard Davey in his *Times* enquiry, *Students in Revolt* (*The Times*, 27–31 May, 1 June, 1968), have found that the principal student extremists there have come from permissive families, and David Reisman is quoted as saying that they are 'the Spockian babies who were picked up', the children who expected instant gratification of their desires. Dr Anthony Storr, in his *Human Aggression*, goes some way towards explaining this point:

> It has been assumed by kindly and liberal persons that, if only children were given enough love and frustrated as little as possible, they would not show any aggression at all. To the surprise of parents who have attempted regimes of maximum indulgence and liberty, the children become emotionally disturbed and often more aggressive than if they had been exposed to firmer discipline. For if parents never assert their own rights as individuals, but invariably submit to the wishes of the child, the latter comes to believe he is omnipotent, and that his every passing whim must be immediately gratified.

Mr Robert Shields, in the *Observer Magazine* (15 September 1968), goes further:

> There is a vast amount of evidence to show that hooliganism and delinquency may be one way by which the adolescent boy carries outside the family a battle with authority which he should have been able to work through with his own father. Typically these youth come from homes in which the father is unable or unwilling to exercise his authority or demand an acceptable standard of behaviour. . . .
>
> When rebelling students, using slogans in place of argument, demand the abolition of money and private property, and an end (once they are in power) to all social and political systems which they dislike, they are not analysing the flaws in contemporary society. Under whatever guise, or in support of whatever cause, they are protesting, their aim is the same – an attack, direct or oblique, on parental standards and parental privileges.

Parental privileges? And, it would seem, parental practice. One group of American psychologists, quoted in *The Times* series 'Students in Revolt', said that 'when students criticize their parents, it is not what they believe, but their failure to practise the beliefs they drummed into their children's ears'. Or, as Dr Benjamin Wolman, Professor of Psychology at Long Island University, puts it: 'What youngsters in many cases are rebelling against is the nihilism they see in their parents' lives – the lack of values, and the empty permissiveness. We must return to the goal of freedom for our minds – not freedom for our impulses.'

Also, those who react to student violence need to consider whether they have an aim adequate to interest the student militant. An editorial in the Oxford undergraduate magazine, *Isis* (7 May 1969), discussing the unrest at the London School of Economics, said:

> There is a madness, if you call it that, among increasing numbers of students in this country. This madness of the L.S.E. majority is no more or less than a desire to go *beyond* analysis of society to *involvement in* changing society. As only the militants offer the latter, they get the support in a crisis. Perhaps they do have an emotional rather than an intellectual appeal.
>
> But who else is atttempting to meet the need of students for a way to contribute towards improving this world not merely improving self?
>
> It would be fascinating to see what the professors and moderates of L.S.E. would come up with if their lives, not only their brains, were as much given to changing society as are those of the radicals. If a sit-in can be dynamite, in Martin Tomkinson's words, a new determination by professors and so far uncommitted students to try to meet, as well as discuss, the world's needs, would be more explosive. They would create the new type of university the age demands.

*　　　*　　　*

The same division of praise and blame between the generations exists in another important section of youth – the hippy movement.

The hippy theory is that if you are soft with yourself, then you will be gentle to others – a theory propagated, as we showed in *The Cult of Softness*, by a modern school of theologians in spite of its being the exact antithesis of the teaching and practice of Christ. How does this theory work out with the 'Freudian proletariat,' as the Flower Children of San Francisco have been called?

Mr Peter Fryer in *Encounter* (October 1967) summarizes their principles as:

(1) Do your own thing, regardless of what anyone else thinks, says or does.
(2) Drop out.
(3) Turn on every straight person you can reach – if possible with cannabis or LSD; if not, turn him on to beauty, honesty, fun and love.
(4) If authority interferes with you, love it to death.

Their dropping out of the world – a *prima facie* sign of affectlessness – is justified by their gentle 'aggression of love'. But parents, it seems, are an exception. 'If you can't turn your parents on, turn on them,' advises the choreographer Jack Henry Moore in an *International Times** editorial (2 June 1967). '. . . It seems that one is going to have to sever relationships with the bastards once and for all so as to have no involvement with their inhumanity.'

'However much it may preach gentleness,' comments Mr Fryer, 'many adolescents find in the Underground a focus for their resentment of repressive fathers, headmasters and police.' He continues:

The Underground promises adolescents both passive resistance and active capacity to shock. You disapprove of the way we speak, our smoking pot, our personal appearance, our late hours, our taste in music? Very well, we'll make our slang an authentic secret language. We'll progress from pot to LSD trips, and from LSD to STP if we can get hold of

* The principal organ of the Hippy 'Underground'.

it, and our entertainments will simulate the mind-expanding effects of our drugs. Our hair will be longer, our skirts shorter, our dress more flamboyant than ever. We'll not merely stay out all night, but campaign for a wide-open, 25-hour city, so as to change 'the waking, sleeping (and no doubt sexual and, consequently, political) habits of life, not only in London but everywhere else in the world where dreary always-sleep-thru-the-dark habits prevail' (I.T. No. 3, 14 November 1966).

As for our pop-music groups, they'll deafen you as they act out the most savage fantasies of violence and destruction, smashing £200-guitars, setting off smoke bombs, starting fires, chopping up television sets and motor-cars and even the stage itself, fighting with each other in near-earnest.

From this, Mr Fryer points out, it seems hardly more than a step to the sleeve note on the *Rolling Stones No. 2* LP, written by their manager Andrew Oldham, which reads:

Cast deep into your pockets for loot to buy this disc of grooves and fancy words. If you don't have bread, see that blind man, knock him on the head, steal his wallet and, lo and behold you have the loot. If you put the boot in, good. Another one sold.

But are the hippies the only ones who are callous? Or are they a reflection of their elders? They are, in the main, the products of comfortable, middle-class homes. They have opted out of the rat race of meaningless materialism which they have seen, and disliked, in us. 'There is in their attitude,' writes Mr Fryer, 'a quiet frightening degree of cultural nihilism and iconoclasm.' But was not that exactly what Mr Con-

nolly found in the most brilliant writers since Baudelaire and which Miss Hansford Johnson finds in the
'humanists' of today? As Mr Fryer concludes:

> They (the hippies) are a glass in which the older
> generation may see its own privatization, its own
> passivity, its own refusal to accept social responsi-
> bility. Older people spend long periods gazing at
> the television screen; the hippies gaze for hours at
> abstract coloured lights. Older people dream of
> winning the football pools; the hippies simply
> dream. Older people smoke tobacco and drink
> alcohol; the hippies smoke pot, go on LSD trips,
> and drift blissfully in 'inner space'. I do not want
> to press the analogy too far; but these similarities
> may help to explain why the older generation pre-
> fers not to look too closely at the Underground and,
> when it does look, hastily repudiates the resem-
> blance and cries vengeance on the *Rolling Stones*.

Or, as the Professor of Poetry at Oxford, Mr Roy
Fuller, said in his Inaugural Lecture:

> Even the offspring of the intelligentsia revolt by
> way of dropping out of education, risk erotic
> alliances, crumbiness of appearance, and so forth,
> perhaps because they see their parents more and
> more obsessed by the gadgets of affluence, and less
> and less convinced that anything can be done by
> way of principle and belief.

REFERENCES

DR ANTHONY STORR: 'Human Aggression' (Allen Lane, 1968), pp. 44–45.

DR BENJAMIN WOLMAN: Quoted in *U.S. News*, 4 December 1967.

'STUDENTS TODAY': (Young Fabian Pamphlet, November 1968), pp. 41, 28–29.

MR ROY FULLER: Inaugural lecture as Professor of Poetry at Oxford University, *Times Literary Supplement*, 20 February 1969.

MR PERRY ANDERSON: *The Times*, 28 May 1968.

7
Is Humanism an Alternative?

'Malraux argues that the contemporary crisis is due to and
has its origins in the demise of Christianity. In a universe
without God, life becomes absurd: death makes the point.'
                                                    JULIAN CRITCHLEY
        in *André Malraux: a profile*, *The Times Saturday Review*,
                                                    18 November 1967.

The retreat from Christianity, then, has been paral-
leled by a retreat from what has, for thirty centuries,
been considered morality, and, as Lord Devlin pointed
out to the British Psycho-Analytical Society, 'One does
not need to be a Christian to discern that, in the
Western world, there is not even a discernible sign
of anything capable of replacing Christianity in the
mind of the populace as the provider of a moral force
vital for the maintenance of good order.' (*The Times*,
10 November 1964.)

In the last decade, humanism, in various forms,
has been put forward as a possible alternative.
'Ethical humanists,' ran an advertisement in *The
Observer*'s personal column recently, 'are happy
humans devoted to living ethical lives based on
rational judgment, with concern for the interests and
welfare of others. If you want to lead a sane, satisfy-
ing life, join the Ethical Society.'

Nudging this announcement were advertisements
from rival atheist societies. 'Humanists who matter
belong to the British Humanist Association,' began
one of them (*The Observer*, 21 January 1968). Each

subtly criticized the others and all called themselves humanists – the 'with it' word for atheist ever since Mrs Margaret Knight used it in her BBC broadcast, 'Morals without Religion', in 1955. This adroit piece of smash-and-grab semantics, which redefined a word originally used to describe Christian scholars like More and Erasmus, in such a way that they would not qualify as humanists at all, seems to have been prompted by the atheists' fear that their philosophy, undisguised, would have little appeal to the public. By adopting the label 'humanist', they infer that they are uniquely human – or even humane; just as the nineteenth-century atheist's disguise as 'rationalist' or 'free-thinker' was meant to suggest that Christians were irrational or in mental chains.

'Humanist,' then, is the label – and 'happiness' is the theme. Mr Harold Blackham, the Director of the high-brow British Humanist Association, coined the slogan 'The Happy Man' for his campaign to raise fee-paying members above the 3,300 mark recorded in early 1967. (*The Observer Magazine*, 16 July 1967.) He printed the 'H for Happy' sign on his notepaper, and sold 'H for Happy' badges, brooches and neck-ties to the faithless. His high-powered Happies (The Humanists Who Matter) moved through the country explaining the Happy Life where 'man is on his own and this life is all'. Their contention is that ethics are better propagated without religion than with it – the philosophy in which Thomas Huxley himself believed while on the London School Board but which he considered impracticable because unlikely to be effective with the masses.

The mass of people seem no more inclined to receive this evangel now than they were in 1870. They refuse to be 'turned on' to atheism by the Happies. As Mr Blackham himself writes, 'Sample opinion polls show again and again the same pattern – the overwhelming majority declare themselves believers in one way or another.' An even larger majority – it was over 90 per cent in the most recent British poll – declare themselves in favour of religious education in the schools, a policy which militant 'humanists' abhor. For even those who make little attempt to practise the Christian code themselves want it to be taught to their children, and only a tiny fraction of the population think that morals can be effectively taught without religion.

In this the majority of the people would seem to be wiser, in their generation, than the children of 'humanist' light. For, as has been seen in earlier chapters, the 'liberal humanists' of the Modern Movement, for all their brilliant gifts, achieved little in the way of personal happiness and did not notably multiply the total of 'ethical lives based on rational judgment, with concern for the interests and welfare of others'. Their aim was to break down the moral inhibitions of the age, and the result, in our own day, has been disastrous. 'If I have no other God,' remarked Dr Austin Farrer, the late Warden of Keble, 'how can I help being God to myself?'

This is exactly what Dr Edmund Leach appears to think man should do. In his Reith Lectures, he stated that, since science offers us 'total mastery over our environment', we 'should behave like gods'. In an article in *The Times* (16 November 1968) he took the argument a step further. Since scientists now had the 'power of creation and destruction', they should 'learn to play God in a moral as well as in a creative and destructive sense'. It is for them to decide what is right and what is wrong, and 'the scientist must be the source of his own morality'.

How would this work out? Dr F. H. C. Crick, the

Cambridge molecular biologist, and Nobel prize-winner, is an articulate atheist. He resigned his Fellowship at Churchill College because a chapel was erected there, and advocates a 'new ethical system based on modern science'.

He suggests that, under this new system, 'a child should not be legally alive until it is two days old and that doctors should be authorized to kill the very old'. 'We need to get rid of our Christian preconceptions and our liberal ones,' he explains. 'Men are not born equal and it is by no means clear that all races are equally gifted. We cannot regard all human life as sacred.' (*Daily Express*, 31 October 1968.)

Earlier, in a discussion between scientists on whether people have the right to have children, Dr Crick said, 'This is taken for granted because it is part of Christian ethics, but in terms of humanist ethics I do not see why people should have the right to have children.' 'Take the suggestion of making a child whose head is twice as big as normal,' he added. 'There is going to be no agreement between Christians and any humanists who lack their particular prejudice about the sanctity of the individual, and who simply want to try it scientifically.'

During this discussion, a group of humanist scientists had suggested that, in order to improve the human race, some compulsory form of eugenics would be necessary. One way, they suggested, would be to put a chemical in the water supply which would sterilize everybody, and give an antidote only to those licensed to bear children. Mr Colin Clark, Director of the Institute of Agricultural Economics at Oxford, who was present, commented that this kind of eugenics had previously led to the Nazi doctrine of genocide. And, come to think of it, Hitler was a man who did think he had to 'play being God'.

Dr Leach concluded his article in *The Times* with a sentence which has a kind of upside down logic about it: 'Unless we teach those of the next generation that they can afford to be atheists only if they assume the moral responsibilities of God, the prospects for the human race are decidedly bleak.' Precisely, but how, if he abolishes God, does Dr Leach plan to make his man-gods as good as they are powerful?

Man can reach the moon, but is unable to live at peace on earth. He is technically able to feed the whole of humanity for the forseeable future, but has not yet developed the unselfishness and concern for others which could spur him to achieve it. To expect him, unaided and unaltered, to 'assume the moral responsibilities of God' is romanticism of the wildest kind.

The fact is that a universe without God is, as Malraux observed, absurd – and humanism has not proved an alternative. Mr Paul Johnson wrote in his London Diary in the *New Statesman* (1 September 1967):

Chesterton thought that when people ceased to believe in God they would not believe in nothing – they would believe in anything. Humanism offered a real alternative, especially in combination with socialist internationalism; but the idea of progress has taken such terrible knocks in the last half-century that it requires a rare degree of intellectual courage – or a self-defeating, irrational act of faith – to convince ourselves that we are not actually going backwards. For most people Chesterton's warning has proved accurate. The young, while despising the short-cuts of their elders, such as organized religion, fall for the new ones with equal gullibility. The spiritual pilgrimage of the Beatles neatly parodies the process. Money, success: found wanting. Then drugs: no good either. Now it's His Holiness the Yogi-man. How long will *he* last?

It would seem that he has already faded, and that the road is clear back to the 'Christianity of Christ', as Keir Hardie phrased it. Under the heading, 'The God that succeeded?', *The Times Diary* (19 November 1968) noted that Arthur Koestler and Ignazio Silone who, twenty years ago, wrote with other disillusioned Communists 'The God That Failed', had now, in the December issue of *Encounter*, both addressed their minds to Christianity. 'In an article called "A Word About Socialism" Silone comes to the surprising conclusion that, in effect, he is basically a Christian after all and that the Lord's Prayer is his basic creed; while Koestler's contribution has Christ, in the first person, discussing the meaning of the Crucifixion with God the Father on his way to Calvary.' 'Has The God that Failed,' asked the Diarist, 'been succeeded by a longer established and more successful deity?'

It is ironical that, just when disillusioned atheists are turning to Christianity, many Christian theologians are suffering a crisis in nerves which is leading them to abandon everything that is distinctive in Christian morals and belief.

REFERENCES

H. J. BLACKHAM: 'Religion in a Modern Society' (Constable, 1966), p. 116. For his 'H for Happy' campaign, see 'Under the sign of the little H' by Ronald Payne (*Sunday Telegraph*, 13 September 1966).

DR. AUSTIN FARRER: From his essay, 'The Christian Apologist' in

'Light on C. S. Lewis' edited by Jocelyn Gibb (Geoffrey Bles, 1965), p. 38.

DR. F. H. C. CRICK and MR. COLIN CLARK: this discussion, which took place at a conference arranged by the Ciba Foundation, is officially summarised in 'Man and His Future' (J. and A. Churchill, London, 1963) and is discussed more fully in our earlier book, 'The Cult of Softness' (Blandford, 1965), pp. 64-75.

8

The Exploitation of Bonhoeffer

'A butcher who advocated vegetarianism would be a rarity; but clergymen with strong atheist proclivities are as common as blackberries.'

MALCOLM MUGGERIDGE

Professor William Barclay, whose new translation of the New Testament is so widely admired, remarks in his commentary on *The Acts of the Apostles* that St Paul always referred to his fellow-Christians as 'the saints'. 'The word used is a Greek word *hagios*,' he writes. 'It is sometimes translated *holy*. But the root meaning of it is *different*. It describes something which is different from the ordinary run of things. Therefore, basically, the Christian is a man who is *different* from the people who are merely people of the world.'

Thus, after urging the Christians in Rome to 'present your bodies a living sacrifice', St Paul continued: 'And be not conformed to this world: but be ye transformed by the renewing of your mind, that ye may prove what is that good, and acceptable, and perfect, will of God.'

The attitude of many present-day Christians – and even of clergymen and theologians – to a world not unlike pre-Christian Rome is exactly the opposite to that of St Paul. They fall over themselves to conform to the world, rather than to transform it – and in the process they are transformed by the world until they are indistinguishable from the secularists among whom they live.

A simple example of this process can be seen in the stampede of clergy of all denominations to praise the magazine, *Playboy*. *Playboy*, created by Hugh Hefner, has been characterized by *Life*, as 'a polished, literate package that urges Americans to enjoy what they have always frowned on: hedonism, which *Playboy* calls the "swinging life"; unmarried sex, which *Playboy* considers a sign of mental health; a suave, pseudo-intellectualism, which *Playboy* presents as sophistication.'

A not untypical article was that about The Sexual Freedom League in *Playboy* for November 1966. The League organizes nude parties and the article quotes various comments by participants. ' "When I went to my first party,' Herb went on, 'I was frankly embarrassed and curious. When couples would start making love on the rug or on the sofa, my eyes almost popped out of my head. . . . Now it all seems so natural." . . . A girl was lounging on the sofa, drink in hand, almost casually fondling the *** *** of the dark-haired man sitting next to her.'

(The asterisks are ours, in place of an adjective and noun printed in *Playboy*.)

Mr Hefner has evolved a 'playboy philosophy' which he outlined in twenty-five consecutive issues of the magazine, the first seven being devoted to sexual freedom. 'Hefner's thesis,' writes *Time* (3 March 1967) 'is that U.S. society has too long and too rigorously suppressed good, healthy heterosexuality. . . . And the villain at the bottom of it all? Organized religion, announced Hefner.'

What was the clerical response to this onslaught? The November 1966 issue, which printed the article on The Sexual Freedom League, opens with three letters from ordained ministers, all of whom find something pleasant to say about the previous issues. 'You are probably aware,' writes the Rev. Charles A. Grube (Presbyterian), 'of the vast number of clergymen who consider your magazine 'must' reading. Thank you very much for articles like the Reverend William Hamilton's *The Death of God* in your August issue.'

The Church became so promising a field that *Playboy* appointed its football editor, Mr Anson Mount, to head up liaison with the clergy. 'As many as twenty clerics and divinity students,' *Coronet* (October, 1966) adds, 'visit *Playboy* offices each week to conduct research into material that Anson Mount has accumulated and to trade ideas. . . . "Hugh Hefner," Mount states, "is the hottest thing in the theological seminaries since Martin Luther." '

Hefner and Mount are invited to address religious groups all over America. *The Living Church* (18 July 1965) reported an occasion when Mount addressed 80 teenagers at Elmshurst, Illinois, along with the Rev. Dr Joseph Fletcher, Professor of Ethics at the Episcopal Theological Seminary, Cambridge, Mass.

> 'It all depends on the situation,' explained Dr Fletcher. 'In certain situations, unmarried love could be infinitely more moral than married love. Lying could be more Christian than telling the truth. Stealing could be better than respecting private property.'
>
> 'Not every pre-marital sex relationship is wrong,' Dr Fletcher told the teenagers. 'According to the new morality nothing is good or bad of itself, but its goodness or its evil depends entirely upon what it does or does not do for persons.'

Mr Anson Mount, a representative of *Playboy* magazine, told the group that the present era, with its relaxation of stringent moral codes and encouragement of individual decisions on morality, presaged a 'golden age of Christianity'.

'We are in the midst of a new reformation and renaissance,' Mr Mount said, and assured the young people they are 'lucky to live in this generation'. He defined the 'moral revolution' of today as the 'replacement of phony values with real ones'.

The teenagers of Elmshurst found it hard to distinguish between the *Playboy* philosophy of Mr Mount and the situation ethics of Dr Fletcher, and indeed *Time* has pointed out that *Playboy* 'exhibits a tendency to situation ethics' of which Dr Fletcher is, according to Dr John Robinson, 'the most consistent exponent'.

Among actions which Dr Fletcher believes to be justified in certain circumstances are murder, adultery, fornication, theft, lying, breaking the law and conspiracy to overthrow a lawfully constituted Government. Indeed, to compile such a list is superfluous, for Dr Fletcher maintains in his *Situation Ethics*, that, within a given situation, anything is permissible, and that in certain situations the 'Christian situationist' would not regard any of these actions as in the category of a choice between two evils. Any of them could represent the 'choice of love' operating with the situation, and therefore would be the highest good, imposing an absolute obligation to be carried out. Moreover, each involves a solely personal decision. 'Every man must,' Dr Fletcher writes, 'decide for himself according to his own estimate of conditions and consequences; and no one can decide for him or impugn the decision to which he comes.' *'This,'* he adds, *'is precisely what this book is out to show.'* (Italics are his.)

On this basis, it is hard to see how anyone could 'impugn' or call in question the decision of Senator Kennedy's assassin. A demented man – or one who believed the Senator was an enemy of his people – could come to the decision that what he had taken was the 'choice of love'. Indeed, his assassin clearly did think that, for in the moment of capture he called out 'I can explain. Let me explain.' 'The appalling thing,' comments *Time*'s essayist, 'is that he really thought he could.'

An even more explicit advocacy of violence as 'a legitimate means by which the Church can help transform the world' came from the American Council of Churches Conference at Detroit in November 1967. *Christianity Today* (24 November 1967) wrote editorially:

One of the twenty-nine work groups was devoted entirely to 'The Role of Violence in Social Change'. Four leaders of this group held a news conference, and three of them thought that snipers in the steeple might one day be a valid tactic. The group's official report reflected this same support of violence, all the harder to believe because it was issued in Detroit, where only weeks before violence had taken the lives of 43, destroyed the property of innocent people and closed businesses, thus stripping many needy people of their jobs. . . .

The New Breed churchmen are groping for a theology of revolution; to few people's surprise, they find that the Bible offers them none (or else at this one point they might consider invoking biblical 'authority'!). Their announced objective is to change the machineries of power in the large

American cities, on the assumption, apparently, that a cadre of church politicians would function as incorrupt and infallible social engineers. Some seem wholly unaware that violence is self-defeating, that violence carries no guarantee of the results its sponsors seek, that perpetrators can easily lose control of it, and that no process of violence can ever provide the new society that mankind needs . . .

The strategy of the New Breed is painfully obvious. Instead of challenging unregenerate man and society with the biblical demand for regeneration, it seeks rapid ways of gratifying the self-interest of the secular spirit. . . . The New Breed is transparently willing – even by violence – to conform the Church to a secular culture in the name of Christian social action.

The secularization of Christianity is being openly advocated by an increasing number of theologians, including Dr Harvey Cox, the co-chairman of the Detroit Conference, whose book, *The Secular City*, is described on the dust jacket as 'a celebration of the new freedom and scope brought to man by secularization'. Dr Cox, who is Professor of Church and Society at Harvard University, defines secularization as 'the deliverance of man first from religion and then from metaphysical control over his reason and his language', and adds:

Secularization simply bypasses and undercuts religion and goes on to other things. It has relativized religious world views and thus rendered them innocuous. Religion has been privatized. It has been accepted as the peculiar prerogative and point of view of a particular person or group. Secularization has accomplished what fire and chain could not:

it has convinced the believer that he *could* be wrong, and persuaded the devotee that there are more important things than dying for the faith. The gods of traditional religions live on as private fetishes or the patrons of congenial groups, but they play no role whatever in the public life of the secular metropolis.

Dr Cox's secular city has two identifying marks – 'profanity and pragmatism'. Profanity he defines as 'man's secular emergence from the temple'. Man has 'come of age' and put away any childish dependence on God. His salvation is to be found in this world, and is achieved by man himself. Pragmatism emphasizes historical acts rather than meaning or being, and therefore lays great stress on politics and social reform as the means of achieving a perfect society. Morality is called 'moralism', piety, 'pietism' and legality 'legalism'.

Dr Cox quotes Camus as 'quietly insisting that man must choose between the tyrant God of Christian theology and being a full man. Having made the choice, man could turn his full attention to striving for justice. . . .' 'I believe,' comments Dr Cox, 'that the choice Camus presents us with is an unavoidable one, and given the choice, as he understands it, we can only choose with him.'

It is ironical that much of this conforming to the world is being carried out in the name of Dietrich Bonhoeffer, the heroic German theologian who was executed by the Nazis as a result of his refusal to conform to the dominant secularism of his day. Dr Fletcher, it is true, considers that Bonhoeffer was insufficiently 'situational' because he turned the maxim that 'the deliberate killing of all innocent life is wrong' into an absolute prohibition; but he nevertheless claims Bonhoeffer as a situationalist, just as Dr Cox considers him a secularist.

It is, of course, true that Bonhoeffer, as early as 1928, warned his congregation in Barcelona that man has not always the good fortune to be able to choose between a right course and a wrong course, but is often faced with a decision in which every possible course has an element of evil in it. This dilemma came vividly home to him when he decided, during the war, to take part in the conspiracy against Hitler, a course which involved lying, deceit and agreement with the attempted assassination. But there remain important differences between his conclusions and those of Dr Fletcher. Bonhoeffer never pretended that lying or murder, for example, were anything but an evil, whereas Dr Fletcher holds such actions, in certain situations subjectively selected by the person concerned, to be the 'choice of love' and so the supreme good.

Similarly, when Bonhoeffer wrote in his *Letters from Prison* that 'man has come of age', he did not mean what many have taken him to mean. While in prison he had opened his mind, perhaps for the first time, to the discoveries of modern science, but he did not assume that, because man had grown to increased physical independence, he had therefore ceased to be the son of a loving Father, or that God or Christ were less central to human life. Quite the contrary. Indeed, the last picture that we have of him, five minutes before he was led away for execution on 9 April 1945, makes this plain. 'Through the half-open door I saw Pastor Bonhoeffer kneeling in fervent prayer to the Lord his God,' wrote the prison doctor. 'The devotion and evident conviction of being heard that I saw in the prayer of this intensely captivating man moved me to the depths.'

Again, Bonhoeffer had in prison observed that the men around him found 'religion' – the self-protective, vested interest of a self-centred church – irrelevant. The contrast he was making in his famous phrase 'religionless Christianity' was between this irrelevant 'religion' and the living Christ. 'The isolated use and handing down of the famous term "religionless Christianity",' said Eberhard Bethge, Bonhoeffer's closest friend and the recipient of the famous letters, in the lecture he delivered in Coventry Cathedral on 30 October 1967, 'has made Bonhoeffer the champion of an undialectical, shallow modernism which obscures all that he wanted to tell about the living God.'

Miss Mary Bosanquet, in her perceptive book, *The Life and Death of Dietrich Bonhoeffer*, wrote that some of the phrases from Bonhoeffer's *Letters* 'have been appropriated and carried away like stones from a half-built church to be used as the foundations of theological superstructures for which he would have disclaimed any responsibility'. Those who have carried them away have often failed to understand the distinction which Bonhoeffer drew between the 'ultimate'–those changeless truths which did not waver from age to age – and the 'penultimate', the way in which those truths might be expressed in any generation. It was of 'penultimates' which he wrote in his *Letters* because 'ultimates' were assumed between associates as close as Bonhoeffer and Bethge, and it was unnecessary to repeat them in such private letters. In her Postscript, Miss Bosanquet concluded:

The task before the Church today, clearly foreseen by Bonhoeffer, is that of becoming fully identified with the modern world without losing her Christian identity. Bonhoeffer is quoted continually as the prophet of identification; that he was equally concerned with the Christian's identity is commonly forgotten.

For him, as for Bethge, the means by which identity was to be maintained was defined by the phrase 'secret discipline', while the demands of identification were summed up in the term 'religionless Christianity', or, more often, 'non-religious interpretation of the Gospel'. Secret discipline meant for him prayer, meditation, common worship, receiving the sacraments; religionless Christianity meant complete openness to the world; it meant being, without any reserve, 'the man for others'.

The *Letters and Papers from Prison*, which are the most widely read and quoted of all Bonhoeffer's works, explore extensively the problems of identification which face the Christian in the present century, while saying little about that secret discipline by which his identity as a Christian is maintained. But what the writer did not say he was living, daily and hourly, and the eloquence of his life counterbalances the reticence of the letters.

Miss Bosanquet pointed out that Bonhoeffer's exploration of 'Christian identity' reached its high point in an earlier period and culminated in his books, *The Cost of Discipleship* and *Life Together*. 'It is a hindrance to the full understanding of what Bonhoeffer was and is,' she concluded, 'that sections of the *Letters and Papers* have so frequently been quoted as though they represented the end of a theological journey instead of its quite tentative beginning. No one can do more than attempt to conjecture how the journey would have continued, but one thing may be taken as certain: the exploration of the means of identification with the world would never have been pursued by Bonhoeffer at the price of his Christian identity.'

It is exactly this loss of Christian identity which appears to be the common denominator of so much of the new theology. Thus, the German 'pioneer' theologian, Rudolf Bultmann, accepts the ideological presuppositions of modern man and uses them as a kind of filter through which to pass the doctrine of the Bible. Modern man, he thinks, will never swallow stories like Christ's miracles or the Resurrection, where an other-worldly God intervenes in a world which is governed by laws of nature. Therefore, the gospel must be de-mythologized. Bultmann left the idea of God intact, but his disciple, Professor Herbert Braun of Mainz, takes his method to its logical conclusion and interprets the word 'God' as a mere symbol of the depth of *Mitmenschlichkeit* – man-with-man-living-together. What of Christian identity remains?

Similarly, the 'God is Dead' theologians in America seem to derive their startling views at least as much from what they believe to be the current state of secular opinion as from any clear belief or disbelief. John Cogley explains in the *New York Times* (3 January 1966):

Some of the 'God Is Dead' professors do not shrink from describing themselves as atheists, a flamboyant touch that makes for headlines if not always for serious communication. They also go out of their way to establish that they are Christian atheists and indicate that they are atheists precisely because they are Christians. However confusing this might appear, their reasoning, based on dialectic and paradox, is considerably more complex than they are sometimes credited with.

Dr Altizer, writing in *The Christian Advocate*, gives some indication of the circuitous pathways of his thought when he says:

> We cannot open ourselves to a new form of faith while remaining bound to the primordial God who has once and for all revealed His word; we will never pass through a new reformation until we liberate ourselves from the God of our Christian past. . . . If faith is now confronting a world in which God is dead, and if this world is present both inside and outside of faith, then faith can speak to this world only by speaking the word of God's death.

In other words, Dr Altizer hopes to win secular man's approval by conforming to a secular view of God, Dr John Bennett, President of the Union Theological Seminary in New York, comments:

> It is hard to take them seriously as theologies at all except as they are protests against the unreality of much 'God talk'. When they say in effect: 'God is dead; long live Jesus,' they would project a kind of Christian thinking that cannot last very long. It would be a miracle if the secular man who cannot believe in God is long able to affirm the centrality of Jesus and to speak of the resurrection in any sense.

Dr Altizer goes further than denying the Resurrection. He denies that God can have any effective relevance in the world of today. 'It is not possible,' he writes, 'for any responsible person to think that we can any longer know or experience God in nature, in history, in the economic or political areas, or in anything which is genuinely modern, whether in thought or experience.'

'The Christian mind,' comments the Anglican theologian, Harry Blamires, 'has succumbed to the secular drift with a degree of weakness and nervelessness unmatched in Christian history.' One wonders, too, whether this loss of nerve is not, in many cases, rooted in a loss of faith – and an unwillingness to make those often costly experiments which, all through history, have tested the obedience of man and confirmed faith in an ever-present God. No one who had honestly put God to the test in his daily life could possibly say with Dr Altizer that we can 'no longer know or experience God . . . in anything which is genuinely modern, whether in thought or experience'.

REFERENCES

PROFESSOR WILLIAM BARCLAY: 'The Acts of the Apostles' (St Andrew Press, 1966), pp. 80–81.

PROFESSOR JOSEPH FLETCHER: 'Situation Ethics' (Westminster Press, Philadelphia, 1966), pp. 37, 74, 5, 65, 101, 104, 110, 130, 143.

DR HARVEY COX: 'The Secular City' (Macmillan, New York), pp. 1, 2, 70, 72.

BONHOEFFER: 'The Life and Death of Dietrich Bonhoeffer' by Mary Bosanquet (Hodder & Stoughton, 1968), pp. 15, 229–231, 254–60, 279–81.

DR JOHN BENNETT and DR ALTIZER: quoted in *New York Times*, 3 January 1966.

HARRY BLAMIRES: 'The Christian Mind' (SPCK, 1963), p. 3.

NOTE

Mary Bosanquet, whose important book we have quoted in this chapter, died of cancer while this book was being prepared for the press. During her last illness she was kind enough to read and correct our chapter.

Part Two

COUNTER-ATTACK

9

The Conflict between Science and Materialism

by Arnold Lunn

I

Many articles have been written about the non-existent conflict between religion and science, far too few about the very real conflict between science and materialism, and far too few Christian apologists are even aware of the fact that in the last half century what little case there was for materialism has been virtually demolished. In this brief chapter I can only outline the results of the experiments in extra-sensory perception. Perhaps the greatest pioneer in this branch of science was Professor J. B. Rhine, Professor of Psychology at Duke University, U.S.A., who has described his experiments in his famous book *The Reach of the Mind*. Professor William MacDougall, in his foreword to Dr Rhine's *Extra-Sensory Perception*, describes Dr Rhine as 'a fanatical devotee of science' who is inclined to suspect Professor MacDougall of 'becoming a renegade' if he finds him reading 'a book on metaphysics or religion'.

Most of Dr Rhine's experiments involved special cards with five different symbols, circle, cross, waves, square and star. His ESP (Extra-Sensory Perception) pack consisted of twenty-five cards, five cards of each of the five symbols.

In tests for *telepathy* the agent Dr Rhine or his assistant, J. G. Pratt, would turn up one of the ESP cards which had been placed face down on a table and look at it and the subject who was being tested would try to name it. In tests for *clairvoyance*, the subject would try to name the card before it had been turned up. In other tests carried out by other experimenters, an attempt would be made to name a card in a special position before the cards had been shuffled and dealt. This would be a test of *precognition*.

Of the many successful tests for telepathy, those in which Sir Gilbert Murray, Professor Arnold Toynbee, the celebrated historian, and his wife took part, were described by Mrs Henry Sidgwick in a report to the Society for Psychical Research as 'perhaps the most important ever brought to the notice of the society, both on account of their frequent brilliant success and on account of the eminence of the experimenters'.

The results of the telepathy and clairvoyance tests by the Rhine-Pratt co-operation were sensational. Mr Stephen Findlay, an agnostic, who in his book *Immortal Longings* examines and remains unconvinced by the evidence for immortality, agrees with the verdict of Dr D. J. West in *Psychical Research Today* that the odds against producing a score of correct guesses as great as the scores achieved in these tests were over a hundred billion to one. And though he himself rejects immortality, he can write: 'The existence of extra-sensory perception like the possible existence of powers of producing the physical phenomena of psychical research is only indirect evidence for survival, or rather indirect evidence against the contention that survival is impossible. . . . Psychical research has at any rate shown us that there is something about the human mind which we cannot explain in exclusively materialistic terms, and this makes it impossible to reply on the materialistic argument against survival.'

Why are we Christians so pathetically slow in exploiting admissions such as this by those who are not Christians?

Mr J. G. Pratt in his book *Parapsychology* writes: 'In the telepathy tests the possibility of some kind of undetected signalling between the sender and the subject had haunted the experimenters throughout the first fifty years. In a test for clairvoyance, in which no one knew what the target was, this danger was automatically eliminated.' It was the results of the tests for clairvoyance at Duke University which particularly impressed Mr Stephen Findlay.

The Rhine-Pratt experiments were continued in England by Dr S. G. Soal and described in his book *Modern Experiments in Telepathy*. Some of these experiments provided evidence for precognition as well as telepathy. In some experiments in which the subject was over 200 miles from the agent, results were obtained, the odds against which being due to chance were more than a billion billion to one.

According to Mr J. G. Pratt, Sir Julian Huxley, who is a convinced secularist, 'was asked in England to nominate the great discoveries of the first half of the twentieth century. Among those he mentioned was the establishment of ESP' (*op cit.* 217). I ask again why don't Christians make use of such admissions, which at least weaken the case for materialism?

Attempts have of course been made by materialists to suggest an explanation of the proved results of

experiments in telepathy and clairvoyance in materialistic terms. Dr Rhine devotes Chapter IX of his book
Extra-Sensory Perception to these attempts.

In the first place if all the cards in an ESP pack
were sending out rays the results would be 'one
unanalysable splotch'. Again whereas energy declines
in intensity with the square of the distance from the
source, 'in the case of experiments with Miss Turner
even more impressive results were obtained at a
distance of 250 miles than in the same room'. And
there are other considerations which tell against the
radiation theory which are discussed by Professor
Rhine. Obviously no materialistic theory in general
or radiation theory in particular could explain precognition.

An important contribution to ESP literature is *A
New Approach to Psychical Research* by Anthony
Flew, Lecturer in Philosophy at the University of
Aberdeen. His attitude of 'resolute but not invincible
scepticism' is ideal for this particular type of research.
The miraculous and abnormal should evoke scepticism but not invincible scepticism, the invincible
scepticism, to quote Mr Findlay, of 'the regrettably
large numbers of scientists who dismiss all evidence
for the paranormal without bothering to examine it'.
And Mr Flew's reluctant conclusion is that 'in the
best work the precautions taken have been adequate,
while the probability calculations seem to be faultless'
and the result is 'to establish the reality of *some* un-
familiar factor'.

In the opinion of Sir Alister Hardy, Emeritus Professor of Zoology at Oxford University, the 'queer
facts' which he feels have been established by
Psychical Research 'show, as I think they do, that the
Materialistic conception of human personality is
untenable'. From which he concludes that 'Psychical

Research is one of the most important branches of investigation which the human mind has ever undertaken'.

It is understandable that scientists should be reluctant to investigate phenomena which are regarded with deep suspicion in conventional scientific circles, but it is far less easy to defend the all but universal failure of Christian apologists to inform themselves about and draw conclusions from the demonstrated results of experiments destructive in their implications of the materialism which is largely responsible for the present decline of Christianity.

II

'Even if science,' wrote the late C. E. M. Joad in *The Recovery of Belief*, 'is no longer a stick with which to beat religion, the plain man's contempt for religion is largely the effect of science.' No, not of science but of Scientism, a Victorian sect of apologists which exploited their interpretation of science in its propaganda for atheism. The present decline of religion is partly, perhaps mainly, due to the lamentable failure of Victorian theologians not only to recognize but promptly to *label* this new sect. In our century the word *scientism* is beginning to come into use, as is also *scientian*, to describe the members of this sect. There is not and never has been a conflict between religion and science, but there is a very real conflict between science and scientism.

Joad's 'plain man' is only too ready to believe in the mythical contrast between scientists, whose conclusions are based on rational deductions from objective evidence, and Christians who accept their dogmas by blind faith. The real contrast is between

Christians who endeavour to convert the sceptic by purely rational arguments that God exists, that the Gospels are historically reliable and that all attempts to explain the origin of Christianity without accepting the Resurrection as proved, have lamentably failed, and the scientian who asks us to accept by blind faith his basic dogma that science has disproved the supernatural. No evidence has ever been offered in support of this dogma. Indeed, the late Professor J. B. S. Haldane, F.R.S., a convinced atheist, conceded that science could not prove that miracles were impossible. 'If God,' he wrote, 'made these laws, I can see nothing unlikely in his suspending them.' (*Science and the Supernatural.*)

In the world of ideas scientians are as dominant today as were theologians in the middle ages, and as subject as were theologians to that particular form of group *esprit de corps* which emphasizes the difference between the group and ordinary mortals. I remember a young man who had taken a degree in science rising at the end of a talk which I gave to a Cambridge club. 'Our approach to these problems,' he said, 'is very different. You are a theologian and I am a scientist.' 'Would you,' I asked, 'maintain that anybody who was recognized to have made a useful contribution to our knowledge of certain aspects of nature appreciated the scientific approach too?' 'Of course,' he replied. 'Well, a book of mine about snowcraft and avalanches was translated into German and French and influenced my election to honorary membership of leading mountaineering clubs in four countries. Now whereas a scientist can write rubbish about religion without inflicting physical damage on his readers, if I had written as irresponsibly about avalanches a reader might have been killed.' As indeed I would have been had I accepted the verdict of a local guide on the safety of a snowslope with the same simple faith that too many readers accept the verdict of scientians on religion. I told him the slope would avalanche and, while he started across the slope, I myself started on a detour. The top layer slid and would have carried him over a precipice, had he not by a marvellous effort somehow got his top ski into the hard layer below, an acrobatic *tour de force* of which I should have been completely incapable.

The greatest contributions to our knowledge of this mysterious universe by theologians and by scientists have been the reward of that intellectual integrity which draws objective conclusions from evidence, but scientists are no more immune than theologians from the temptation to be unduly influenced by the wishful thinking which attaches undue importance to any evidence which appears to point in the desired direction. As indeed is candidly admitted by Sir Alister Hardy, F.R.S., in his Gifford Lectures, published under the title *The Living Stream*. Here is what he writes about scientific impartiality:

> Some people, thoughtless people, imagine that all scientific research must be conducted with a cold impartiality. That is the ideal, but it is often, I would say usually, impossible; and we must recognize it. If what we are testing concerns only the physical world we may achieve such an aloofness; even here, however, if we have invented a pet hypothesis, which by intuition we feel must be true, we are in danger of falsely imagining ourselves to be getting the results we expect. The scientist who has vision, who has fertile ideas, is not unlike the artist in having a certain, perhaps misplaced, affection for the children of his creative thoughts.

The proportion of theologians who have been ready to examine, if only for the purpose of adequate refutation, beliefs or phenomena difficult to reconcile with orthodoxy has been far greater than the proportion of scientists who are equally ready to examine phenomena which conflict with the dominant philosophy of modern science, materialism.

Even scientists who reject materialism have, with rare exceptions, been reluctant to investigate phenomena the reality of which is difficult to reconcile with scientific orthodoxy, such as the phenomena associated with Psychical Research. Characteristic was Thomas Huxley's reaction to the Dialectical Society's invitation to join the committee appointed to investigate and, as originally hoped, to expose as fraudulent the psychical phenomena produced by David Hume. Hume, who believed that he had a mission to demonstrate immortality, never accepted payment and once declined an offer of £2,000 for a single seance. 'A highly desirable characteristic of Hume's mediumship,' wrote the distinguished scientist Lord Rayleigh, 'was the unusual opportunity allowed to the sense of sight. Hume always objected to darkness at his seances.'

The committee of thirty-four members, including fellows of scientific societies, physicians and barristers, were reluctantly compelled to report that they had witnessed paranormal phenomena such as 'heavy bodies – in some instances men – which rise slowly in the air and remain there without visible or tangible support'.

The Dialectical Society were so dismayed by the Committee's report that they refused to publish it, but after the committee had published the report at their own expense, the Society invited Huxley to join the committee and continue the investigations.

Huxley refused. He could have pleaded that he was too busy. Instead he made a contemptuous reference to Spiritualism as if the acceptance of certain paranormal physical phenomena necessarily involved the acceptance of Spiritualism*. 'Supposing the phenomena to be true,' he wrote, 'they do not interest me.' What he might well have written was, 'Supposing the phenomena to be genuine they are impossible to reconcile with scientific orthodoxy and I dare not expose my faith to such a trial'. Huxley in fact behaved much the same as those Biblical fundamentalists who refused to examine fossils lest the fossil record should upset their faith in the literal accuracy of Genesis.

Sir Alister Hardy's gentle criticisms of 'scientific impartiality' may well have been reinforced by the reluctance of most scientists even to examine the case for extra-sensory perception. He devotes Chapter IX of *The Living Stream* to the reasons 'why most scientists have an aversion for these matters', reasons which he considers inadequate. Sir Alister was convinced by the card guessing experiments of Dr Soal and Professor Rhine that clairvoyance and even precognition have been proved. He quotes Professor C. D. Broad: 'There can be no doubt that the events described happened and were correctly reported; that the odds against chance-coincidence piled up to billions to one.' Sir Alister Hardy adds: 'More recently still has come psycho-kinesis, the alleged influence of the mind upon falling dice which is again seemingly established by the scoring of the same sort of degree of probability above a chance result as may be found in other fields.'

* Thanks to Sir Arthur Conan Doyle I attended some seances which he arranged with some of the more notable of contemporary mediums. My experiences reinforced my belief that paranormal phenomena have been demonstrated but I never accepted Spiritualism. A.L.

Sir Alister fully realizes that the acceptance of these phenomena as proved 'conflicts with one or more of the basic limiting principles', that is with the dominant philosophy in modern science. It is understandable that scientists should be reluctant to argue in favour of beliefs, the advocacy of which might prove damaging to their careers. Professor J. B. Rhine in *The Reach of the Mind* maintains that 'the fear that retards the scientific acceptance of psi (Extra-Sensory Perception and Psycho-Kinesis) is a social one: the fear of losing caste in one's profession. . . . Many scientists have experimented with ESP and PK in secret. Sometimes we hear about these efforts only indirectly unless it happens that only chance results are obtained. It is safe, even creditable to publish negative findings. But occasionally we learn of successful and valuable experiments only to be told that 'for professional reasons' no report will be published. 'My family has to eat,' said one of these experimenters. 'My institution would object,' said another. 'Every member of my department would criticize me, and I am in line for the chairmanship,' said another.

III

'It is difficult,' writes Mr Harry Blamires in *The Christian Mind*, 'to do justice in words to the complete loss of intellectual morale in the twentieth-century Church,' a pessimistic verdict which is endorsed by Professor E. L. Mascall who in *The Secularisation of Christianity* comments on 'the failure of nerve which has stampeded so many contemporary theologians into a total capitulation to their secular environments'.

A striking example of this all but 'total capitulation'

is the lamentable failure of Christians, with a few notable exceptions, to adopt an attitude of critical interest in the evolutionary controversy. It would be disastrous for Christianity to be identified with *any* particular school of evolutionary thought, but discreditable that Christians should not have continued to point out that scientists were as divided as are Christians on the issues involved, and that the evolution itself was accepted by many scientists for theological rather than for scientific reasons.

Darwin had been anticipated by Buffon, Lamarck and Erasmus Darwin in the promulgation of the evolutionary theory, and his immense success was partly due to the fact that his purely materialistic explanation of evolution was published at a time when a majority of scientists were looking for an alternative to what Huxley called 'the untenable theory of special creation'.

The real difficulty of the evolutionary theory is the missing chains rather than the missing links in the geological record. Dr Lecomte Du Noüy, whose scientific discoveries were recognized by awards from the Franklin Institute of Philadelphia, the French Academy and the Institute of Lausanne, and who insists that 'it is almost impossible nowadays not to be an evolutionist', points out in his famous book *Human Destiny* (1947) that so far as the evidence of the fossil record is concerned, 'each group, order, or family seems to be born suddenly and we hardly ever find the forms which link them to a preceding strain. When we discover them they are already completely differentiated. Not only do we find practically no transition forms, but in general it is impossible to authentically connect a new group with an ancient one.'

Huxley, in his 1862 address to the Geological

Society, said, 'In answer to the question "What does an impartial survey of the positively ascertained truths of palaeontology", that is the study of the fossil records, "testify in relation to the common doctrines of progressive modification?" that is evolution, I reply, "It negatives those doctrines, for it either shows no evidence for such modifications or demonstrates that such modifications have been very slight".' None the less, Huxley accepted evolution as the only alternative to the doctrine of special creation.

In the introduction to a controversial correspondence between Douglas Dewar, a special creationist, and H. S. Shelton, an evolutionist, four evolutionists were quoted who accepted evolution. They all, to quote one of them, Professor D. M. S. Watson, accepted evolution not because it could be proved to be true but because 'the only alternative, special creation, is clearly untenable'.

Evolution, in fact, was accepted for theological and not for scientific reasons. It is no more scientific to accept evolution because one rejects special creation than to reject evolution because one accepts special creation. It has been said that scientists had to accept evolution because they could see no reasonable alternative, but surely there is nothing unreasonable in the agnostic alternative, the admission that the origin of species is an unsolved problem. 'The only statement,' wrote that great biologist Reinke, 'consistent with her dignity that science can make is that she knows nothing about the origins of man'. (*Der Türmer* V. Oct. 1902.) Whereas the early evolutionists were convinced that further research would be rewarded by new evidence for evolution, the agnostic attitude has increased in later years. 'A student,' wrote Sir Albert Seward, F.R.S., 'who takes an impartial retrospect soon discovers that the fossil record raises more problems than it solves. We want to know where we are; faith, as Dr Bateson says, has given place to agnosticism.' (*Nature*, 26 April 1924.)

There would also seem to be a revival of what may be defined as Wallace-evolution. Wallace, who co-operated with Darwin in promulgating the theory of Natural Selection as an evolutionary agent, did not believe that natural forces alone could account for the ascent of man. He suggested 'that there were three stages in the development of the organic world when some new cause or power must necessarily have come into action. The first when the first living cell was created, the second when the animal kingdom separated from the vegetable kingdom, and the third at the creation of man.'

Among the moderns Sir Alister Hardy could be described as a Wallace-evolutionist, for he certainly does not believe that evolution can be explained solely by material processes. He tells us that he is 'far from being an orthodox Christian', but in his book *The Living Stream* he writes: 'It was not so much the fact of evolution that was so destructive of faith, but the growing fear, fanned by the pronouncements of scientists, that it could only be a materialistic process. That is why I have devoted so much time in these lectures to showing that the hitherto generally accepted mechanism of a natural selection by only the *physical* side of the environment is by no means the whole of the evolutionary story.'

Incidentally any critic who still retains a prejudice in favour of discovering what a man believes before attacking his beliefs can assume that I am a Wallace-evolutionist.

Science, like Christianity, has its fundamentalists who accept their basic beliefs by faith and who reply to criticism of those beliefs by personal attacks on their critics, and just as an occasional theologian has denounced Christian critics who did not accept his conception of theology as anti-Christ, so evolutionary fundamentalists often assume that critics of evolution are anti-scientific. I remember H. G. Wells' remark about a book which had recently appeared, 'I suppose you are pleased to see a scientist fouling his own nest.' On the contrary, what gives me pleasure is to find a scientist, such as Sir Alister Hardy, reconstructing a faulty nest. What is urgently needed is a scientific approach to religion.

The Science of Life contains a characteristic example of evolutionary fundamentalism. 'There is today,' wrote the authors, Sir Julian Huxley and H. G. Wells, 'no denial of the fact of organic evolution except on the part of manifestly ignorant and superstitious minds.' Does Sir Julian really believe that Larousse, one of the most famous publishing houses not only in France but in the world, would have commissioned a 'manifestly ignorant and superstitious' writer to undertake the editing of the volume of the *Encyclopédie Française* devoted to *Les Etres Vivants, Plantes et Animaux*? The concluding essay in this volume is by the editor, Paul Lemoine, former Director of the National Museum of Natural History at Paris, and is entitled 'Que valent les théories de l'évolution?' and here is Lemoine's answer: 'The theories of evolution, in which our student youth was cradled, constitute a dogma which all the world continues to teach: but each in his speciality, zoologist or botanist, comes to the conclusion that none of the available explanations are adequate.' Lemoine then analyses the difficulties of reconciling evolution with palaeontology and biogeography, and concludes: 'Il resulte de cet exposé que la théorie de l'évolution est impossible. . . . Cela il faut avoir le courage de le dire,

pour que les hommes de la génération future orien-
tent leurs recherches d'une autre façon.' (It results
from this summary that the theory of evolution is impossible. . . . It is necessary to say this in order that
future generations may orientate their researches in
another fashion.)

'Il faut avoir le courage.' Yes indeed, for as Thomas
Dwight, Parkman Professor of Anatomy at Harvard,
wrote, 'The tyranny of the *Zeitgeist* in the matter
of evolution is overwhelming to a degree of which
outsiders have no idea. Not only does it influence
(as I admit it does in my own case) our manner of
thinking, but there is oppression as in the days of
the Terror. How very few of the leaders of science
dare to tell the truth concerning their own state of
mind.' My quotation is from *Thoughts of a Catholic
Anatomist*.

'That explains it,' some readers may comment with
relief. But does the fact that Sir Arthur Keith regarded
evolution as 'a basic dogma of rationalism' (*Darwinism and its Critics*) explain why Sir Arthur was an
evolutionist? The truth is that evolution is *de fide*
for atheists whereas Christians are free either to accept
or reject evolution. The Catholic Church allowed evolution to be taught as a hypothesis from the first. Any
intelligent discussion of a scientific problem must
concentrate on the arguments advanced and not on
the alleged motives of the arguer.

Evolution is not only a 'basic dogma of rationalism'
but of modern thought, and it is never easy to revolt
against the tyranny of fashion, social or intellectual
as the case may be. This natural reluctance explains
the uncritical acceptance by most Christians of a
purely materialistic explanation of evolution. I believe
myself that our prestige today would be higher if we
had been identified from the first not with the accep-

tance or rejection of evolution, but with the demand for a truly scientific approach, and a refusal to accept as coercively proved what was probable but by no means certain. Again, we should never have acquiesced in the superstition that there were only two alternatives, special creation and a purely materialistic theory of evolution. We, at least in our schools, should have insisted on Wallace's theory of evolution being examined.

What is even more difficult to understand is our failure to expose the most dishonest of scientific bluffs, the implicit claim in the title of Darwin's book that the *evolution* of species explained the *origin* of species. For the ultimate origin of all species on a lifeless planet is the problem to which atheism has no key.

No atheist denies that there was no life on our planet in its original molten condition, and that the real 'origin of species' is a cell capable not only of self-nourishment but also of passing on life. 'A representative cell', wrote Professor J. B. S. Haldane, 'contains over ten thousand, but less than a million distinct chemical substances. When there are ten thousand biochemists in the world, it will be time to ask them to make a cell.' (*Science and the Supernatural*.) Even if chemists did succeed in making not only a living cell, but a cell with the power to reproduce itself, the problem of the *spontaneous* generation of a cell on a till-then lifeless planet would not be solved.

Christians have not the slightest reason to be intimidated by science. 'Let us,' then, to quote the concluding words of Sir Alister Hardy's *The Living Stream*, 'go forward to reclaim the ground that has been lost in the world through a false belief that science points only to materialism.'

REFERENCES

PROFESSOR J. B. RHINE: 'The Reach of the Mind' (Faber, 1948), p. 145. 'Extra-Sensory Perception' (Faber, 1935).

STEPHEN FINDLAY: 'Immortal Longings' (Victor Gollancz, 1961).

D. J. WEST: 'Psychical Research Today' (Revd. edition, Penguin, 1962).

J. G. PRATT: 'Parapsychology' (W. H. Allen, 1964).

DR. S. G. SOAL and BATEMAN, F.: 'Modern Experiments in Telepathy (Faber, 1954).

ANTHONY FLEW: 'A New Approach to Psychical Research' (Watts & Co., 1953).

SIR ALISTER HARDY: 'The Living Stream' (Collins, 1965), pp. 239, 156, 240–2, 264, 288.

PROFESSOR C. E. M. JOAD: 'The Recovery of Belief' (Faber & Faber, 1952).

PROFESSOR J. B. S. HALDANE: 'Science and the Supernatural', pp. 35, 307.

HARRY BLAMIRES: 'The Christian Mind' (SPCK, 1963), p. 3.

PROFESSOR MASCALL: 'The Secularization of Christianity' (Darton, Longman & Todd, 1965), p. 282.

LECOMTE DU NOÚY: 'Human Destiny' (Longmans, 1947).

SIR JULIAN HUXLEY and H. G. WELLS: 'The Science of Life'. (Cassells, 1931).

PAUL LEMOINE: Encyclopédie Française, Vol. 5 (Larousse).

PROFESSOR THOMAS DWIGHT: 'Thoughts of a Catholic Anatomist' (Longmans, 1927), p. 20.

SIR ARTHUR KEITH: 'Darwinism and Its Critics (C. A. Watts, 1935).

HERDER CORRESPONDENCE (Verlag Herder, 78, Freiburg, Germany).

10

Why Christianity Survived

by Arnold Lunn

How did Christianity survive the Crucifixion? Far too little thought is given to this key problem by those who deny the Resurrection. Few indeed of those who attack Christianity have the historical imagination to recreate the world into which Christ was born and thus to realize the necessity to find some plausible explanation for what was so fantastically improbable, the conversion of the Roman world to a new religion which originated in a despised colony. It is all but impossible to suggest a plausible parallel in our own times, but what the Christian missionaries achieved in the first centuries of our Christian era may be rendered easier to understand by a fictitious example. If an Indian mystic had persuaded himself and his disciples that he was an incarnation of God, if he had been shot by the English at the time of the Indian Mutiny, if his disciples, demoralized by his death, had been transformed into dynamic missionaries by their conviction that their master had risen from the dead, and if the missionaries of this Indian sect had penetrated to England and converted all but a trivial minority to their faith, their achievement would have been no more surprising than what Christian missionaries actually achieved in the Roman Empire. To a civilized Roman the prediction that his traditional religion would vanish without trace, and that the chief priest of a Jew-worshipping religion would one day rule in Rome would have seemed no less grotesque than a prediction that one day the established religion of England would be not Christianity but the worship of an Indian saint would have seemed to a Victorian Englishman.

Whether Christ did or did not die on the Cross, one thing must be admitted even by those who deny the Resurrection. Only those whose faith in the Resurrection was uninfected by the slightest hint of doubt could have had the faintest hope of making converts even in Palestine, to say nothing of the Roman world.

I cannot do more in this chapter than outline the case for the Resurrection, which is the subject of my book *The Third Day* and of my controversial correspondence with C. E. M. Joad, *Is Christianity True?* Both books are out of print, but I would be happy to believe that some readers of this book might get my debate with Joad from the library, if only to realize how easily the case against the Resurrection can be met and refuted.

Let me begin by a brief and therefore inadequate summary of the evidence for the authenticity of the Gospel record. In the first two centuries of our era manuscripts were usually written on papyrus, a frail material, with the result that hardly any contemporary papyruses survive from that era. In the case of the Gospels a special effort was made by the persecutors of the Church to destroy manuscript copies. Even so, the earliest Gospel manuscripts which we possess are far nearer in time to the date of composition than those of *any* classical author, the nearest of which – a manuscript of Virgil – being written 350 years after the poet's death. For Euripides the interval is as much as 1,600 years. On the other hand the great vellum uncials of the New Testament were written some 250 years after the Gospels were actually composed, and we have fragments of St John which palaeographers assign to the first half of the second century.

What is admitted, even by sceptics such as D. F. Strauss, who maintained that the Gospels are legendary accounts written many years after the events which they purport to describe, is that, to quote Strauss, it was *certain* 'that the same four gospels which we still possess were recognized by the Church, and repeatedly quoted as the writings of those Apostles and of those disciples of the Apostles, whose names they bear, by the three most eminent ecclesiastical teachers – Irenaeus in Gaul, Clement in Alexandra, and Tertullian in Carthage.'

The first duty of the elders ordained by the Apostles to preside over the churches entrusted to their care was a written record of our Lord's life and teaching. Nobody could deny the necessity for Gospels in the primitive church, and those who maintain that the Gospels we now possess are in important respects different from the primitive Gospels have to produce a plausible explanation of how a forger could have obtained credence for a forgery. Those who assume such an alteration to be possible know little, as Dr Salmon justly remarks, of the conservatism of Christian hearers. St Augustine tells us that once when a bishop ventured to substitute, while reading the chapter about Jonah's gourd, St Jerome's 'hedera' for the established 'cucurbita', such a tumult was raised, that if the bishop had persevered he would have been left without a congregation.

Those who, like Strauss, maintain that the Gospels are 'legendary accounts', that they are works of fiction, have yet to produce plausible attempts to explain

how obviously unpractised writers, apparently unaware of the principles which even inexperienced
fiction writers observe, could have created characters,
quite apart from the central character, as convincing
as the most famous characters in the greatest master-
pieces of fiction. Pilate, for instance. How vividly he
comes to life in the few verses in which he appears.
The prototype of reluctant agnostics: 'Pilate saith
unto him, "What is truth?"' A man too easily intimidated by the implied threat of 'If thou let this man
go, thou art not Caesar's friend', but who dramatized
the impact of our Lord in a gesture which has been
immortalized in our language. 'When Pilate saw that
he could prevail nothing, he took water, washed his
hands before the multitude, saying, "I am innocent
of the blood of this just person."' All his hatred
and contempt for the Jews who had blackmailed him
into condemning their victim, whom he knew to be
innocent, emerges not only in the title he wrote and
put on the cross, JESUS OF NAZARETH THE KING OF THE
JEWS, but also in his uncompromising rejection of
the Jewish protest, a rejection in words which have
passed into our speech, 'What I have written, I have
written.'

It is not only Pilate who comes alive in the Gospels,
but his wife in the one brief reference to her, the wife
who 'sent unto him saying, "Have nothing to do with
this just man, for I have suffered many things today
in a dream because of him."'

I find it difficult to understand how anybody, let
alone anybody who has himself tried to write fiction,
could remain unconscious of the *Ring of Truth*, to
quote the title of a book by an Anglican author, Canon
J. B. Phillips, in the Gospels. The Gospels are full
of loose ends and unsolved conundrums which no
fiction writer would tolerate. No fiction writer capable

of inventing that wonderful story of the woman taken in adultery, a story which ends with the sublime picture of our Lord writing in the dust, could have refrained from telling us what Jesus wrote. St John does not tell us. Why? Perhaps because he could not see.

His Gospel ends: 'And there are also many other things which Jesus did, the which if they should be written every one, I suppose the world itself could not contain the books that should be written.' St John's Gospel occupies 33 pages in my Bible, and, when one recalls the many volumed biographies of worthies who are destined to be forgotten before many years have passed, one cannot help regretting what Canon Phillips calls 'the maddening brevity' of *all* the Evangelists.

And to quote Canon Phillips once again, 'One thing is perfectly clear: these men were not in a conspiracy together or they would have been careful to avoid minor contradictions and discrepancies.'

Few critics are so foolish as to maintain that the Gospels are entirely fictitious. In their vocabulary the precious word 'interpolation' is handy when they wish to dismiss, without evidence or argument, any text which refers to miracles. Most sceptics admit that Jesus lived, that he was crucified and that his disciples believed in his Resurrection. Why then was not the body of Jesus produced by the Pharisees from the tomb in which it had been laid? Why was the tomb empty? In *The Third Day* I discussed the explanations put forward by leading agnostics, but within the limits of my space here it is best to confine myself to the only explanation which deserves serious consideration, the explanation put forward by the Sanhedrin. They were not only an intellectual élite, but also practical politicians who knew that *their* explanation had to satisfy their contemporaries and, if need be, to stand up to the critical examination of *contemporary* witnesses, whereas modern explanations put forward by men of the study are not exposed to the risk of contemporary cross-examination. *The Sanhedrin knew what they could get away with,* and their attempt to account for the empty tomb was obviously the least unconvincing of all those which they passed in review. And what they asked their contemporaries to believe was that the disciples had stolen the body of Jesus from the tomb.

If the disciples had done so, they would have been confirmed in what they sadly believed – that Jesus had died the death of a deluded prophet. Why then should the disciples, who panicked in Gethsemane, have conspired to impose on the world a new religion which they themselves believed to be false, and have broken with their church and risked the same death as their master in defence of a monstrous and superfluous lie? 'I readily believe,' wrote Pascal, 'those witnesses who get their throats cut.'

Finally since it is even more important to do what we can to prevent the *perversion* of Christians than to effect the *conversion* of secularists, we must discuss the claim of those modernists who reject the miracles in general and the Resurrection in particular, to call themselves Christians. Modernist Christianity of this extreme variety is not a genuine religion. It is a *pis aller* for those who have lost their faith and who are reluctant for emotional, or perhaps in the case of some ecclesiastics also for practical reasons, to break with Christianity. Has any atheist or agnostic been converted to Christianity by this non-miraculous Christianity? As a young agnostic I re-read the Gospels with particular care, for I had been sent down from Oxford for failing in an examination, long since abolished, in the rudiments of Holy Scripture, and was anxious to resume my studies in Oxford. The difference between God and Man is infinite, and the parables did not seem to me *infinitely* more beautiful than some recorded utterances of saints and mystics. My agnosticism was not shaken by what Christ said, but I had an uncomfortable feeling that I was reading the accounts of eye-witnesses when they described the Resurrection.

I have counted the verses in the Gospels which describe miraculous events. They amount, by my reckoning, to 856 verses out of the total of 3,747 verses, that is 22.47 per cent. Why should a modernist claim to be Christian on the authority of documents all but three-quarters of which are in his view fictitious? Why should witnesses who are completely unreliable when they record what Christ did be trustworthy when they record what Christ said?

It is impossible in a short chapter to do more than to awaken the interest of readers who have never studied the historical evidence for the Resurrection, and to hope that they will read further on the subject. *Ring of Truth* and *Who Moved the Stone?* by Frank Morison are available in paperback editions.

REFERENCES

THE THIRD DAY by Arnold Lunn (Burns & Oates, 1945).

IS CHRISTIANITY TRUE? by Arnold Lunn (with C. E. M. Joad) (Eyre & Spottiswoode, 1933).

D. F. STRAUSS: 'Das Leber Jesus'.

PILATE: John XVIII; 38, XIX; 12, Matthew XXVII; 24, John XIX; 19, 22, Matthew XXVII; 19.

CANON J. B. PHILLIPS: 'Ring of Truth' (Hodder & Stoughton, 1957).

FRANK MORISON: 'Who Moved the Stone?' (Faber, 1944).

I I

An Apology for Apologetics

by Arnold Lunn

I

In a posthumous fragment of a book published by *The Month* under the title *Proving God*, the late Monsignor Ronald Knox wrote: 'On the whole we are in the age of unreason . . . Sir Arnold Lunn . . . pilloried this mood of our age a quarter of a century back when he wrote *The Flight from Reason*, expecting angry disclaimers from every side. And the public reaction, on the whole, was "Why not?" '

Nearly forty years have passed since the book in question was published in 1930, and the flight has almost become a rout. Psycho-analysis, which in itself is neither basically irrational or anti-rational, has been exploited by the irrationalists in their determination to ignore any reasons which a man may advance in defence of his beliefs. Objective truth is dismissed as unobtainable and all that is of interest about a man's beliefs are the irrational influences which led him to certain conclusions; but no irrationalist is consistent for, if he were, he would be forced to deduce from his own premises the conclusion that all that is of interest about his conviction that objective truth is unobtainable is the irrational influences which led him to this conclusion. So too Dr J. B. Watson, a major prophet of Behaviourism, the main thesis of which is that the thinking processes are merely the mechanical by-products of mechanical activity, not only expected his readers to take his thinking processes seriously but was at some pains to advise them on the conduct of their lives, though as Dr Mores observed in his preface to the *Symposium of Behaviourism* 'why a Robot should advise other Robots what to do is another of the mysteries Behaviourism has not solved.'

There is, of course, as Dr Mores remarked, a public which is 'delighted to hear that the old gods are dead and the old beliefs with their checks and balances and controls are without validity,' and that men are at last free 'to liberate their libidos'. The Oxford of my youth not only provided education but also influenced standards of behaviour, as no doubt modern Oxford does in spite of the fact that 'Logical Positivism', which was merely a variant of 'Behaviourism' and which dismissed all ethical judgements as 'pseudo-concepts', was popularized by the Wykeham Professor of Logic in modern Oxford. Professor A. J. Ayer, F.B.A., has held this chair since 1959, the year in which he published his famous book *Language, Truth and Logic*, in which he wrote: 'If I now generalize and say "stealing is wrong", I produce a statement which has no factual meaning – that is expresses no proposition that can be either true or false.' I am told that Professor Ayer, when asked in the course of a discussion whether the statement 'Hitler was wrong to murder Jews' had factual meaning, conceded that some ethical judgements were *not* pseudo-concepts – those, we may be sure, by which his own private life is influenced.

The anti-rational mood of the age has admittedly aggravated the difficulty of converting sceptics by rational argument, but even if the anti-rationalists had been incomparably more successful than they have been, it would still be the duty of those who are capable of effectively stating the rational case for Christianity to continue to use the reason God gave them in defence not only of God but also of reason itself. To abandon by implication the claim that Christianity can be rationally defended is implicit, if not explicit, apostacy. Fortunately the number of those who can be influenced by rational argument is far greater than the more timid of our Christian defeatists suspect. Every experienced apologist knows from his own personal contacts, in person or by letter, that the rational case for Christianity is an important, and in many cases the most important factor in the conversion of sceptics and also, be it noted, in preventing the perversion of doubting Christians. A professor at a well-known American University told a friend of mine that he would certainly have left the Church had he not read a book which he named. There are many such cases.

The influence of rational argument in conversion varies from convert to convert. In many cases it has no influence whatever. Some converts who have been mainly influenced by their own deep need for religion were regretfully convinced by secularist propaganda that the reality of the supernatural had been decisively disproved, by science, and in their case the return to the practice of religion has been rendered possible by the discovery that the secularist case can be met and refuted by rational argument. Even if they themselves cannot follow the argument or are uninterested in the rational case for the religion, for which they feel an urgent need, the example of converts whose intellectual powers are admitted by their opponents may prove decisive.

At the other extreme there are the converts from dogmatic and ill-informed secularism, who far from feeling any need for religion are strongly prejudiced against the Christian creed because of the Christian code, particularly in matters of sex. Christians, we are often assured, are influenced by wishful thinking, and it would be considered very indelicate if we hinted that an atheist might be prejudiced against Christianity by the wishful thinking which is reluctant to believe in posthumous sanctions.

The main difficulty with most secularists is to persuade them to examine the case for the supernatural. Canon J. B. Phillips recalls in the *Ring of Truth* 'hundreds of conversations with people, many of them of higher intellectual calibre than myself, who quite obviously had no idea of what Christianity is about.' He concluded that 'they knew virtually nothing' about the New Testament. The Resurrection 'the most important event in human history is politely and quietly by-passed. For it is not as though the evidence had been examined and found unconvincing; it had simply never been examined.'

When I read this I was reminded of my old friend and sparring partner, the late C. E. M. Joad, in his time a famous broadcaster and popularizer of secularism. He challenged me to discuss Christianity in a series of letters, published in 1932 under the title *Is Christianity True?* Joad, like the modern secularists, to whom Canon Phillips refers, reminded me of the character in *The Man Who Was Thursday*, who knew all about Christianity because he had read it up in two works, *Religion the Vampire* and *Priests of Prey*. And yet Joad died a practising Christian, largely, so he told me, because of our correspondence. If Joad could be convinced once he was compelled to meet the rational case for Christianity, are we Christians perhaps not to blame for the fact that we have failed to induce the majority of our contemporaries even to examine that case?

It is not as if the case had been badly presented. I have studied the apologetics for many systems of thought, and it is not merely because I happen to be a Christian that I am convinced that no philosophic or political system has been more effectively presented. The apologists have done *their* job, it is what may be called the public relations aspect of Christianity which is open to criticism. Why is it that it is only the exceptional school of all those who profess to give a Christian education which ensures that all pupils, save those most resistant to education, leave school aware of the fact that there is a rational case for the Resurrection, and that some at least of their pupils will, in later life, make an active contribution to the reconversion of countries once Christian? In schools in which apologetics is taken seriously the proportion of pupils who in later life continue to practise their religion is increased, and some at least, admittedly a small minority, will become active propagandists for Christianity. I taught apologetics for three semesters, before the last world war, at Notre Dame University, Indiana, famous for its football team but far more concerned to produce laymen who could make a useful contribution to the counter-attack on the atheism which was advancing rapidly in America as in our own country. One of my pupils, who kept in touch with me, helped to convert ten secularists within a few years of leaving Notre Dame.

When I first met my pupils I asked them to put on paper how they would defend the Resurrection in an argument with an atheist. Their replies, with one exception, were lamentable, and yet all of them had been educated in Catholic schools. When I congratulated the student who had produced the only creditable answer, he replied that he had discussed the Resurrection with Mr Christopher Hollis, who had been on the Faculty the previous year, and that Mr Hollis had made 'the Resurrection sound really interesting'. What, however, is difficult to understand is how any competent teacher could fail to arouse interest in the most fascinating of all historical controversies, the origin of Christianity – fascinating because of its bearing on infinitely the most important of all issues, the nature of man. Is man nothing but an agglomeration of matter, destined after some three score years and ten to final extinction, or is he a rational being with responsibility for his actions and with an immortal destiny? It is indeed easy to interest any intelligent man in theology if theology is presented in some such terms. Margaret Crawford in an obituary of a famous Alpine guide, Hilti von Allmen, which was published in the *British Ski Year Book for 1966*, recalls his excuse for being four hours late for an appointment with her. He had been lunching with a mountaineer who had this eccentric taste for theology and who, to Hilti's surprise, could 'make theology sound wonderfully interesting'.

Our first problem in this increasingly secular world is to convince the victims of secularism that supernatural events, which no materialistic philosophy can explain, have occurred and are still occurring. If there had been no miracles since the first decades of Christianity, the task of the Christian apologist would indeed be difficult, but this is very far from being the case. The evidence for some modern miracles is so strong that even a convinced atheist such as the late Professor J. B. S. Haldane wrote of them: 'Still one or two of the more surprising Lourdes miracles, such as the immediate healing of a suppurating fracture of eight years' standing seem to me to be possibly true and, if so, very remarkable and worth investigating, although if they were shown to be true they would not prove the particular theory of their origin current at Lourdes.' (*Science and the Supernatural*.)

I would agree that modern miracles might legitimately be regarded as evidence for the supernatural in general rather than for any particular religion. An Anglican could accept the authenticity of some of the Lourdes miracles without accepting Roman Catholicism just as I believe that Canon Phillips gave a truthful and reliable account of two supernatural phenomena, though I am not an Anglican, on page 90 of his book, from which I have already quoted. Canon Phillips tells us that a Bishop to whom he mentioned this perplexing experience replied, 'This sort of thing is happening all the time'.

The first objective of the Christian apologist, whether he is teaching a class, writing a book or discussing Christianity with a sceptical friend, is to arouse interest in the supernatural in general rather than in Christianity in particular. Many who no longer believe in the reality of the supernatural are reluctant materialists, and easy to interest in any evidence which awakens in their mind the suspicion and, perhaps, the hope that there are indeed phenomena which materialism cannot explain. There is, as we have seen, an increasing tendency to accept extra-sensory perception and telepathy as proved beyond reasonable doubt, and the relevance of these discoveries to philosophy in general and materialism in particular is, at least, a fascinating subject for discussion. There have certainly been instances where the acceptance by a former agnostic of psychical phenomena as proved has been the first step towards accepting the supreme miracle of the Resurrection. On the other hand Haldane's atheism was unshaken by the fact that he was inclined to accept as proved cases in which a medium 'becomes possessed of knowledge by abnormal channels'.

When I taught apologetics I invited discussion of

psychical phenomena, for the modern apologist must be familiar not only with the modern evidence for miracles, the Lourdes miracles for instance, but also with all phenomena which weaken the case for materialism.

'When I was in the seminary,' an American priest recently remarked to me, 'we all read Belloc and Chesterton, but apparently it is not "with it" for a modern seminarian to be interested in apologetics. The Church, it would seem, must concentrate exclusively on social welfare.' I think, or at least hope, that my friend was unduly pessimistic, for it is as essential for a Church as for a political party to state its case effectively, and fatuous to hope for converts if we are not prepared to provide potential converts with a rational case for our beliefs. A well-known Catholic who would like to turn what is left of the Church militant into the Church pacifist, wrote me a letter of mild rebuke. 'I far prefer,' he wrote, 'St Francis de Sales' methods to yours.' 'So do I,' I replied, 'and if I were a saint I would not need to argue, for as that great rationalist Hilaire Belloc was the first to insist, "Holiness has about it a power like none other. It convinces, attracts and confirms. It also reveals."' Saints do not need to argue but many have been converted to Christianity by ordinary sinners who have taken the trouble to master and to present the overwhelming case for Christianity.

II

The first problem to be solved by those who are making a serious attempt to organize an effective counter-attack to triumphant secularism is to induce those who are as uninterested in Christ as in Buddha,

and in some cases considerably less interested, to hear
what we Christians have to say in defence of our
bizarre beliefs. Orthodoxy is not news. The erratic
ecclesiastics who led the campaign for what they
called 'The New Morality' received plenty of publicity, but 'Bishop disapproves of fornication' is, as
yet, an unlikely headline in our morning paper. I
have, however, been encouraged by the fact that many
people who would never attend a lecture given by a
Christian will put in an appearance at a debate between a Christian and an atheist and that people who
would never read a book by a Christian will read a
book consisting, as did my books with the late Cyril
Joad and J. B. S. Haldane, of a controversial correspondence between a Christian and an atheist.

I fully realize that most of those who follow such
debates are merely confirmed in their previous beliefs,
but the debates are worthwhile for the occasional
convert whom one does make. Joad himself, for instance, and Louis Budenz, the former Communist
editor of the American *Daily Worker*, who returned
to the Church and wrote in *The Brooklyn Tablet*
of our debate: 'His Christian consideration for me
as an opponent and his rapier-like exposure of Communist philosophy made a deep impression on me.'

Of my own contributions to apologetics I believe
the most useful to have been *Science and the Supernatural*, an exchange of letters with the late Professor
J. B. S. Haldane, for a secularist who has been
induced to read a defence of Christianity can always
buttress up his scepticism when confronted by an
argument which he himself cannot refute by attribut-
ing his failure not to the strength of the case for
Christianity but to the dialectical skill of the Christian
apologist, and by assuring himself that the Christian's
specious arguments could be demolished by an equally

effective apologist for atheism. No such consoling explanation of the strength of the Christian case is possible in the case of a book which contains within its covers the case for and the case against Christianity argued by competent apologists for Christianity and atheism respectively. Mr Ronald Clark, Haldane's biographer, was in general sympathy with Haldane's scepticism, but the most he could claim for Haldane was that 'though neither opponent achieved a knock out, J.B.S. won on points'. On the other hand a reviewer of a book of mine in *The Times Literary Supplement* (10 October 1968) maintained that in this controversy I 'got much the better of the scientist, J. B. S. Haldane'. That Haldane certainly failed to demolish the case for the supernatural could only be attributed to the strength of that case, for Haldane was obviously my intellectual superior. 'He became,' writes Sir Peter Medawar in his introduction to the Haldane biography, 'one of the three or four most influential biologists of his generation. . . . In some respects he was the cleverest man I ever knew.'

Atheists have been curiously successful in convincing the ill-informed that modern science has rendered it impossible for any intelligent man to believe in God or miracles, and my correspondence with Haldane was worth while if I had done no more than extract from him the admission that there was no scientific argument against the possibility that God might exist or that, if He did exist, He might permit the miraculous interference with the natural order.

Haldane's letters are indirect evidence of the pernicious influence of atheism on a brilliant mind. He could write unmitigated rubbish as, for instance, when he wrote that he 'was willing to consider the possibility of exceptions to it', 'it' being 'the statement that $2 \times 3 = 6$', thereby flatly contradicting what he himself had said on p. 38 of the same book, 'Thus if I say that $2 \times 3 = 6$, I mean something which is absolutely true, and would be so even if no example existed to demonstrate it.' Even more significant are the misrepresentations of which atheists, whose intellectual integrity one would hesitate to doubt, are sometimes guilty in their attempts to defend any scientific theory which seems to provide an alternative to the existence of God. Darwinism was and is regarded as *de fide* for such atheists. 'Darwinism' I do not, of course, equate with evolution, but with that particular explanation of evolution for which Darwin was responsible, the theory that Natural Selection is creative and responsible for new species. 'We have now,' wrote Thomas Dwight, Professor of Anatomy at Harvard University, 'the remarkable spectacle that just when many scientific men are agreed that there is no part of the Darwinian system that is of any great influence, and that, as a whole, the theory is not only unproved, but impossible, the ignorant, half-educated masses have acquired the idea that it is to be accepted as a fundamental fact.'

It is, of course, easy to refute anti-Darwinists if you can only contrive to create a confusion between natural selection as a *fact*, and natural selection as a *creative agent*. In our joint book I quoted from Haldane's *Possible Worlds* his remark that 'The assertion is sometimes made that no one has ever seen natural selection at work.' One would have to be very foolish to make such a ridiculous assertion for every epidemic is a case of natural selection. The fittest survive. Haldane continued by citing the case of a part of a wood in which light birches had been replaced by dark pines, with the result that the white moths which showed up against the dark pines were gradually being exterminated. Sir Julian Huxley who collaborated with the late H. G. Wells in producing *The Science of Life* quoted this passage and added a few words of his own, the words I have italicized, to Haldane's 'The assertion is sometimes made that no one has ever seen natural selection at work *in the production of new characters.*' In my review in *The New English Review* of *The Science of Life* I quoted the passage, as misquoted by Huxley and Wells, and asked where were the new characters which had allegedly been produced. White moths are gradually exterminated – granted – but the moths which survive are still white.

The next development was an indignant letter from Haldane in which he complained that the words 'in the production of new characters' had been added to what he actually wrote, and that I had attributed to him 'an obviously silly remark'. After I had apologized to the readers of my review for assuming that a quotation by Darwinists from a Darwinist did not need to be checked, Mr Wells wrote an angry letter to *The New English Review* in which he stated that the words added to the quotation from Haldane had 'manifestly been inserted for greater clearness'. What Sir Julian Huxley and Mr Wells had in effect achieved was unintentionally to expose what was 'obviously silly' in the original passage, the silliness in Haldane's original argument being implicit rather than explicit.

I have never heard of any Christian being perverted by Haldane's argument but I know of two cases where the book proved helpful in the conversion of the readers to Christianity. Lord Longford in his *Born to Believe* wrote: 'Arnold Lunn's controversy with Haldane removed my sneaking suspicion that in a real showdown there would be materialist questions which the man of religion would not face.'

I am sorry I did not make more impression on Haldane for I had the greatest admiration not only for his intellect but also for his exceptional courage. 'It seemed hardly natural,' said one of those who served under him in the First World War, 'to be as fearless as he was'. And it was not only in war but in a series of dangerous and painful experiments on his own body that Haldane gave evidence of outstanding courage.

III

It is regrettable that the rational defence of Christianity should be described as 'apologetics', derived from *apologetikos*, a Greek word to describe those who 'speak in defence of', but which has unfortunate verbal resemblances to 'apologise', and this perhaps partially explains the fact that Christian apologetics is so often apologetic in tone, and there is too little counter-attack.

Christianity is a very old religion, and the sins of Christians, particularly during the centuries when the Church was politically powerful, have provided atheists with material for attack, but what use have Christians, with occasional exceptions, made of the disastrous results of atheism in power in Soviet Russia? For fifty years atheism has been the official creed of Soviet Russia. 'In school,' wrote a leading Party theoretician, L. F. Ilichev, 'the foundations are laid for scientific world outlook. In the near future religious ideology in our country will have been eliminated.' (*Kommunist*, 1964. No. 1.)

Religious persecution was a shameful episode in Christian history, but atheists have no hope of drawing smug contrasts between their record and ours, for incomparably more political heretics were executed in atheistic Soviet Russia in half a century than religious heretics in many centuries. The reviewer in *The Times Literary Supplement* (3 October 1968) of Mr Robert Conquest's *The Great Terror* quoted and did not question the estimate that 20 million were executed in Stalin's purge in the 'thirties.

It is characteristic of our apologetics that whereas most people have heard of the Church's persecution of Galileo, only an all but negligible minority are aware that scientific, as well as political, heretics have been savagely persecuted in Soviet Russia. In our debate, Haldane was rash enough to refer to scientists who had been burnt alive 'at the instigation of the clergy', whereas there is *only one* case, in the long history of the Church, of a scientist getting into trouble with the Church because of his scientific views. Galileo had the misfortune to be writing at a time when the reigning Pope, unlike his immediate predecessors, disagreed with the theory that the earth goes round the sun, a theory which was first published in the Christian era by Canon Copernicus in a book which was dedicated to the reigning Pope. None of the nine Popes that followed raised any objection to the Copernican theory. 'In the generation which saw the Thirty Years' War, and remembered Alva in the Netherlands,' wrote that distinguished mathematical philosopher, Professor A. N. Whitehead, F.R.S., 'the worst that happened to men of science was that Galileo suffered an honourable detention and a mild reproof before dying peaceably in his bed.' Haldane, of course, could not cite a single case of a scientist who had been executed because the Church objected to his scientific views.

In a letter to *The Times* (24 April 1933) Sir Bernard Pares, Professor of Russian at the University of London, gave details supplied by Professor Tschernavin, 'a distinguished ichthyologist', of the fifty-one scientists in his own branch of science, known to himself, in prison. 'Twenty-five have been shot and twenty-six deported in three years.' (1930-1932.) Victor Serge, a former communist, describes in his book *Russia Twenty Years After*, the effects of what he describes as 'managed science'. 'Geologists have been imprisoned,' he writes, 'for having interpreted subsoil qualities differently from what was wanted in high places'. 'There was plenty of grotesquery about "Leninist surgery" and "Stalinist mathematics".' Eugene Lyons adds, in his *Assignment in Utopia*, 'The roster of scientists, historians, Academicians, famous engineers, technical administrators, statisticians arrested at this time reads like an encyclopaedia of contemporary Russian culture.'

How many educated Christians, I wonder, even realized that scientists have been ferociously persecuted in atheistic Russia? How many of those who are actually teaching apologetics have drawn attention to the contrast, so flattering to Christianity, between the high respect with which the most conservative of the Christian Churches treated science and the savage persecution of science by the atheistic government of Soviet Russia?

If Marxism had been a triumphant economic success, it might be possible to justify the loss of intellectual freedom as a necessary and purely temporary price to be paid for the increased prosperity of the working classes, but the Berlin wall is the answer to such claims. For in this case the East German problem would be to prevent too many West German workers attempting to enter the workers' paradise, but the workers in West Germany are content to stay where they are and the East German problem is not to control immigration but to prevent emigration. When Adam and Eve were expelled from Eden, a cherubim 'with flaming sword' prevented any hope of returning, but the Marxist variety of cherubim stands guard at the Berlin wall, ready to shoot anybody who attempts to escape from the Marxist Eden.

IV

From the contemporary decline of Christianity one could argue either that the case for Theism has been refuted or that Christians in a nominally Christian country have been lamentably ineffective. It is not as if it were difficult to interest a teenager or an adult in his ultimate future. Does the grave end all? Many of those who have been infected by the secular climate of the modern world are both surprised and deeply interested to discover that there is, after all, a strong case for the supernatural. A politician who heard me make this point in a discussion said, 'You're quite right. Christopher Hollis did a lot of good in the House of Commons because it gradually got round that the Resurrection was one of his subjects, and many members tackled him and were deeply interested.' Hollis's experience was not unique. I too have often met people who had received what is flatteringly described as a Christian education and who were yet both startled and relieved to discover that there was a rational case for Christianity.

The first problem is to establish effective contact with those who have ceased to be and with those who have never been Christians, a problem which is insoluble if Christianity is to degenerate into a ghetto whose inhabitants never discuss Christianity with those outside the Christian ghetto. It is tacitly assumed that the last thing which a Christian who has achieved distinction in a secular activity would wish to discuss is Christianity. I remember a broadcast interview

which began, 'Your main interests, I take it, are mountaineering and ski-ing?' and the embarrassed pause
which was the reaction to my reply, 'No, my main
interest is the defence of Christianity.' Beyond a factual correction I made no further reference to my
'main interest' for it would obviously be improper
to make irrelevant remarks about religion in the discussion of a purely secular problem, Olympic-
amateurism, but the rapid advance of secularism
could, I believe, be checked, if Christians were ready
to use legitimate openings for a friendly discussion of
these supreme issues. It is very easy to interest people
in the evidence for the supernatural, and what is more
surprising, some, at least, of the more brilliant atheists,
so far from resenting an attack on their position seek
personal contact with those who hold such odd views.
That brilliant novelist, H. G. Wells, was also an atheist and after reading an article in which I had vigor-
ously attacked some of his anti-Christian propaganda,
he asked me to lunch, and gave me a signed copy of
one of his own books. George Orwell had no use for
the Catholic Church but he too gave me one of his
books, and we often lunched together and discussed
a problem, to which he himself admitted that he had
found no solution, the problem of how to provide
an inducement to encourage men who no longer believed in God or immortality to behave decently.

In general, secularists have a mild contempt for
Christian defeatists who seek to conciliate the secular
world by playing down the supernatural in Christianity, but often have a certain respect for their more
militant opponents. *The Literary Guide* is the organ
of those who like to be described as 'rationalists' but
in its issue of July 1965 it wrote: 'Sir Arnold Lunn
is a man after my own heart. He is a swashbuckling
survival from the great days of controversy before

everybody became so mealy mouthed.' What is certain is that the advance of atheism will not be checked by 'mealy mouthed' Christians. When, therefore, we read an ill-informed and intemperate attack on Christianity we should not be content to register an indignant protest, but ask ourselves how far we Christians are responsible for the ignorance of the critic in question. What efforts have we made to enlighten him? Do we take every reasonable opportunity to draw the attention of those who misrepresent our beliefs or our behaviour to the facts?

Here is a case in point. I have read with great pleasure and profit Mr Ronald Clark's excellent studies of the Huxleys and his biography of J. B. S. Haldane and I found his book *The Victorian Mountaineers* very useful when I was writing *A Century of Mountaineering*, which the Swiss Foundation for Mountain Research had commissioned me to write as their tribute to the centenary of the Alpine Club. Mr Clark was, however, as ill-informed about Victorian ecclesiastics as he was well-informed about Victorian mountaineers and his suggestion that the Victorian clergy 'were doing their best to maintain a belief in the cosmology which the awkward scientists were destroying with unnerving ease' was derived from the folklore of Victorian Freethinkers. No scientific discovery is embarrassing to Christians whereas some recent discoveries are all but fatal to materialism.

My first reaction to Mr Clark's contemptuous references to the Victorian clergy was to make no comment, lest I should be attacked for dragging religion into a book about mountaineering, but I realized that it would be shameful for one who had criticized other Christians for timidity in defending their beliefs himself to fail when put to the test. So I devoted a paragraph to correcting Mr Clark's representation of the ecclesiastical attitude to science. Having by this time recovered my nerve, I also wrote a chapter on the influence of mountain beauty on the religion of mountaineers. I pointed out, *inter alia*, that 'one reason why the Alpine pioneers were more intelligible than the moderns in interpreting their mountain philosophy is that they did not attempt the impossible task of trying to construct an Alpine theology without mentioning Theos.' I waited with some apprehension for the review in the *Alpine Journal*. Actually few reviews have given me greater pleasure. The reviewer, Sir Edwin Herbert, President of the Club, selected for special praise the passages which I feared might provoke rebuke, the fact for instance that men have found in the mountains something 'which is beyond time and space: a fourth dimension; in one phrase the Logos who is God. All will unite in thanking Sir Arnold Lunn for the manner in which he has refreshed our thoughts of

The Chief Things of the Ancient Mountains
And the Precious Things of the Lasting Hills.'

An increasing number of those, not only in my country but also in America, who have received a good education know little more about Christianity than about Mohammedanism, and for this reason any legitimate opportunity for correcting false statements about Christianity in the kind of periodical which they do read be taken. There is always the possibility that a man who discovers that he is grossly mistaken about at least one aspect of Christianity may be sufficiently interested to seek further information about what was once the religion of his country.

We are faced today by a concerted and organized attempt to eliminate what little is left of the Christian influence on our country, but there is, as yet, no attempt to organize a counter-attack. Inadequate use is, for example, made of television, that most effective medium for propaganda. A member of a television team which was interviewing me about ski-ing was asked what he thought of the presentation of Christianity on television. 'Too bland,' was his reply. There are, of course, exceptional television performers who are anything but 'bland' on the subject of Christianity, but I have seldom heard on television an effective and confident attack on materialism.

The Ecumenical movement has been of real value in promoting friendly relations among the different churches, but has been of little value so far as the counter-attack on secularism is concerned. Ecumenism, to quote from a paper by an Anglican, Mr Edward Smyth, 'now seems bent on establishing agreement based on a watered-down version of Christianity as the lowest acceptable common denominator. It is thus the very opposite of militant and may well become scarcely Christian in the New Testament sense of the word.'

Debating, either verbal or written, is among the best mediums for publicity for militant Christianity, for it attracts not only Christians but atheists. I recently challenged Professor Julian Huxley to a written debate. 'My controversy with the late J. B. S. Haldane,' I wrote, 'was accepted by the Catholic Book of the Month Club of America and my controversy with the late G. C. Coulton, *Is the Catholic Church Anti-Social?* by Burns & Oates, publishers to the Holy See. We Catholics know that we have nothing to fear from such controversies. Are secular humanists equally confident?'

Sir Julian declined my challenge, but referred me to the Secretary of the British Humanist Association.

Their General Secretary had expressed in the correspondence columns of *The Tablet* (7 December 1968)
a keen desire for 'dialogue', a fashionable word for
what is hoped will prove a discussion between a sceptic
and an intimidated Christian, but my letter to the
British Humanist Association remained unanswered
for ten days. When I rang up to know whether it had
arrived, a very courteous General Secretary informed
me that he had passed on my challenge to various
Humanists, among them Professor A. J. Ayer, whose
fundamentalist reaction recalled that of Biblical fundamentalists, for he insisted that there was nothing
left to debate. The General Secretary, however,
assured me that he was still searching for a 'humanist',
who would not evade that dialogue for which in the
columns of *The Tablet* his Association had proved
so eager. He mentioned one possible name. 'I'm
afraid,' he said, 'he is rather combative.' And with
this touching but deserved tribute to my essentially
uncombative nature the conversation closed.

At the time of writing, the B.H.A. has failed to
produce anyone willing to accept my challenge.

REFERENCES

PROFESSOR A. J. AYER: 'Language, Truth and Logic' (Victor Gollancz,
1964).
J. B. S. HALDANE: 'J.B.S. The Life and Work of J. B. S. Haldane' by
Ronald Clark (U.S.A. Coward McAnn, 1969) Introduction, p.
211.
LORD LONGFORD: 'Born to Believe' (Jonathan Cape, 1953), p. 100.
SIR JULIAN HUXLEY (with H. G. WELLS): 'The Science of Life'.
(Cassell 1931.)
THE MAN WHO WAS THURSDAY by G. K. Chesterton (J. W. Arrow-
smith, 1908. Reprinted as paperback, Penguin, 1967).

12

Faith by Experiment

by Garth Lean

In the second part of his Gifford lectures, published under the title *The Divine Flame*, Sir Alister Hardy considers the relations of science and religious experience. He writes:

> For a long time many, perhaps most, philosophers and theologians have felt that, since science and religion are poles apart, the very idea of a scientific approach to theology is quite absurd. I agree that science has no more to do with the *essence* of religion than it has to do with the emotional appeal of art. Nevertheless a scientific theology, a natural theology in Lord Gifford's sense, could, I believe, by encouraging research and marshalling its facts in a systematic way, demonstrate to the scientifically thinking world that there is overwhelming evidence (1) to show that religious experience has played and can play an important part in human behaviour, (2) that there is a certain consistent pattern in the records of such experiences and (3) that on so many occasions men and women have achieved, by what they call divine help or grace, that which they, and others who knew them, would have regarded as beyond their normal capabilities.

Such a scientific theology could only emerge, in Sir Alister's view, when 'a vast natural history of religious experience' has been brought together – a process already begun in the case of primitive peoples by modern social anthropologists but not seriously attempted with regard to civilized peoples. He points out that, in the animal world, a science of ecology only became possible after an immense collection of facts by naturalists, and foresees the same process in this study of human behaviour.

Sir Alister maintains that 'the study of the religions of the less sophisticated peoples by those social anthropologists who had truly got to know their subjects – and not just evolved theories about them from their arm-chairs – has shown that the outstanding character of such elementary faiths is a feeling of being in touch with some Power beyond the self from which, with suitable approaches, they can draw help and confidence in their daily life'. He is confident that the study of modern man would lead to much the same conclusion.

This view was supported by Sir Frederic Bartlett, the Professor of Experimental Psychology at Cambridge, in his Riddell Memorial Lectures:

I confess that I cannot see how anybody who looks fairly at a reasonable sample of actions claiming a religious sanction can honestly refuse to admit that many of them would not occur, or at least that it is highly improbable that they would occur in the forms in which they do, if they were simply the terminal points of a psychological sequence, every item in which belonged to our own human, day to day, world. I am thinking not of the dramatic and extraordinary actions which people who write books about religion mostly seem to like to bring forward. They are rare any way. I remember the ways of life of many unknown and humble people whom I have met and respected. It seems to me that these people have done, effectively and consistently, many things which all ordinary sources of evidence seem to set outside the range of unassisted humanity. When they say 'It is God working through me', I cannot see that I have either the right or the knowledge to reject their testimony.

Miss Barbara Ward, in her *Faith and Freedom*, points out that religious experience is no less valid as evidence than any phenomenon on which science bases its conclusions. She writes:

The firmest proofs of religion are rooted in the nature of reality – in the necessities of reason, in the underivative character of such concepts as truth and goodness. Since, however, the Western mind has in the last century become more and more accustomed to think of proof in the pragmatic terms of modern science – a thing being 'true' if it can be shown to work – it is perhaps worth remembering that even here in the sphere of pragmatic proof faith and science conform to a similar pattern and claim a comparable validity. The world which science lays bare, in its capacity as weigher and measurer, is one of soundless, colourless impulses of energy which under given conditions appear to behave in certain ways. This clearly is not reality as such for, at the very least, reality must be allowed to be coloured, scented and noisy – qualities which do not appear in the scientific picture. Yet science can predict up to a point how, under given conditions, this queer universe of energy will behave.

Proceed in a given way to set up your experiment and the experiment will work; and, on the theory of probability, repeat the same conditions and the experiment will work again. Thus, even if science cannot say what reality is, still less say whether its abstracted picture is 'true', it can say that certain methods of handling reality work.

What is perhaps not very generally realized is that if this is the full extent of science's claim to lay bare reality, religion can proceed with much the same degree of certitude. The saint can say: 'This universe I tell you of, in which God's being and energy and love fill all reality and in which the base of your own soul is anchored in the Source of Being, may seem to you very far removed from the colourful material reality which you meet every day. But is it stranger than the colourless, sound-less energies of science? Stranger than the notion that you are sitting this moment upon an inter-section of physical impulses? Than that reality is a dance of electrons? The energy of God and the energy of nuclear power are equally remote from daily experience.'

But, some will say, we can prove the existence of nuclear power by setting up immensely complicated experiments, processing matter through them and at the other end receiving a predictable explosion. 'Then,' the saint continues, 'I say that the experi-ments of the religious life work in exactly the same way. We, the scientists of goodness, tell you that if you will take the raw materials of your all too human mind and body and process them through the laboratory of detachment, humility, prayer and neighbourly love, the result will be the explosion into your life of the overwhelming love and know-ledge of God. Do not think you can know God except by hearsay unless you submit yourself to this experimental process, any more than you can produce nuclear fission without an Oak Ridge or a Harwell. But we promise that if the experiment is carried out under clinically pure conditions – as it has been in the life of the best and purest of mankind – then the result is scientifically certain. The pure of heart shall see God. That statement of fact is as experimentally certain as that H_2O is the constitution of water, and it is proved by the same experimental means.

If science is known by result – and this is in fact where its certitude rests – so, too, are the truths of religion. The experimental tests of religion are more delicate and unstable than those of science, for the raw material – the heart of man – has not that implicit obedience to the law of its own nature which is observable in metals or minerals or even living tissues. Inconveniently but gloriously, it has a free and unconditioned element. Again and again, in the laboratory itself, the experiment is botched. Yet where it is triumphantly concluded – in a Buddha, in a Lao-tse, in a St Francis of Assisi, in a St Peter Claver or a John Woolman – the experimental proof of religion shines forth with a light no less clear than that of science.

Sir Frederic Bartlett, as we have seen, thought that this experimental proof of religion was no less evident in the lives of 'unknown and humble people' who were anything but saints, and Sir Alister Hardy suggests that any individual can make the experiment for himself. He writes:

Experiment to see if it works. However unlikely it may seem to one from one's rationalistic upbringing, try the experiment of really imagining that there is some element that one can make contact with beyond the conscious self. Have that amount of faith – and see . . . Somehow, in some extraordinary way, I do believe that there is a vast store of wisdom and spiritual strength that we can tap in this way – something which is of the utmost importance to mankind.

While Sir Arnold Lunn, as he has explained, came to belief through a study of the rational case for Christianity, I began my own journey from agnosticism to belief through experiment. It was represented to me, while studying law at Oxford, that such an experiment was possible, that I should accept God as a 'working hypothesis'. I initially protested that I did not believe in God, but had reluctantly to admit that, if God in fact existed, my own belief or disbelief in Him did not alter that fact. I decided, in the spirit of experiment, to give as much of myself as I knew to as much of God as I understood, and to begin by taking as my aim the absolute standards of morality – honesty, purity, unselfishness and love – which are outlined in the New Testament. I soon saw that much must go out of my life – and much else come in – if I were to make the experiment in anything remotely approaching the 'clinically pure conditions' of which Miss Ward writes. I set to work to put right those things – thefts and relationships, for example – which I could myself put right, trusting that God would forgive and rectify those things which I had no power to put right.

As my experiment proceeded, I began to notice a change of motive within myself which was beyond my ability to effect. The change in conduct and character which resulted was definite enough – and obvious enough to others – to convince a dozen other undergraduates that it would be worth their making a similar experiment – with similar results. In the years since then, I have observed such experiments in literally thousands of people in many countries, and have seen the influence of such changes in social, industrial, national and even international situations.

The Christian life – for from these initial experiences I moved on to a knowledge of the saving power of Christ – is a continuous series of experiments or acts of faith where the Christian is out of his depth, utterly dependent on God's intervention to give him the wisdom, courage or material assistance needed in situation after situation. To maintain the 'clinically pure conditions' in which each experiment can be made, a careful watch on motives is needed, plus a dedication and self-discipline beyond the demands of mere duty or of what one can get away with. Sin, it is said, binds, blinds, deadens and multiplies – which is why the affectless society is the inevitable end result of a self-indulgent generation. 'Sin,' goes the rough and ready, but practical definition, 'is anything which comes between you and God or between you and someone else'; for we are at any moment no closer to God than to the person from whom we are most divided.

One kind of experiment which the secularists have been unable to explain away is the act of faith in pursuance of the belief that 'where God guides, He provides'. A well-attested example of this principle at work was that of George Muller, who died in 1898 and whose story is told in *The Life of Trust: Being a Narrative of the Lord's Dealings with George Muller*, a book which is quoted at length in William James' *The Varieties of Religious Experience*.

Muller, in the course of his life, distributed two million copies of the scriptures, equipped several hundred missionaries, built five large orphanages in

America in which he educated 121,000 orphans. He received and administered a million and a half pounds sterling, and left at the age of eighty-six an estate worth £160. Muller never ran up bills and never bought supplies for which he could not pay on the spot. God provided, but only just what was needed and only just in time. Muller wrote:

> Greater and more manifest nearness of the Lord's presence I have never had than when after breakfast there were no means for dinner for more than a hundred persons; or when after dinner there were no means for the tea, and yet the Lord provided the tea; and all this without one single human having been informed of our need.

When supplies came in slowly Muller always felt that this was a trial of his faith. When his faith and patience had been sufficiently tried God would send more:

> And this has been proved, for today was given me the sum of £2,050 of which £2,000 are for the building fund and £50 for present necessities. It is impossible to describe my joy in God when I received this donation. I was neither excited nor surprised; for I *look out* for answers to my prayers.

Through the centuries, both before and since the time of George Muller, Christians of all communions have had a similar experience to his. Mother Teresa of Calcutta is one of numberless Roman Catholics who have no doubt that 'faith and prayer' works in the world of today. Born in Albania, she went to India in 1929, working as a Loreto nun. In 1948, single-handed and with no resources whatever, she began to care for the destitute dying whom she found in the streets and dust-bins of Calcutta, and between 1952 and 1966 alone, she and her Missionaries of Charity – who now number more than three hundred – picked up 18,435 desitute who were dying, and breathed life back into over half of them. Her work now includes the care and rehabilitation of lepers and the care of thousands of children, and has spread from Calcutta to dozens of other Indian cities. She receives no official aid or grants. 'The Lord never lets us down,' she says. 'Notoriously the religious orders are nowadays short of vocations,' wrote Malcolm Muggeridge in the *Catholic Herald* (16 May 1969), 'nor has permitting lipstick and the wearing of mini-skirts served to reverse the trend. On the other hand, the Missionaries of Charity are multiplying at a fantastic rate: their Calcutta house is bursting at the seams and each year three or four new enterprises are started, in India and elsewhere. As the whole history of Christianity shows, when everything is asked for, everything – and more – is accorded; when little, then nothing. Curious when this is so obvious that today the contrary proposition should seem to be more acceptable.'

Another example of this principle at work in the modern world, is provided by the Evangelical Lutheran Sisterhood of Mary at Darmstadt, Germany, some account of which is given in *Realities* by Basilea Schlink, one of the two founders of the Sisterhood, which is now established in several countries.

'This book,' she writes in *Realities*, 'does not deal theoretically with the idea of a God who works miracles. It is a factual report of that which the Living God has actually done.' It tells how, starting with nothing in the years after the war, the Sisterhood acquired land, built a spacious centre, church and guest houses, and fed themselves and their guests entirely through 'faith and prayer'.

For seventeen years, the sisters have spent no money on personal needs, such as soap, toothpaste, shoes, linen, towels or handkerchiefs. These items, like their building materials, have arrived as needed. Until nine years ago, they sometimes bought food to supplement what they were given or grew in their gardens; but in 1959, they decided, in a desire to be ever more dependent on God, to buy no food. Day by day, week by week, exactly on time, but sometimes only a few minutes or an hour before a community of 80 and their guests would sit down to table, enough would arrive for the needs. Basilea Schlink remarks that any advertisement for a cook would have to read:

Wanted, one cook. No money available for food or supplies, but generous prayer-support from all the Sisters. Menus usually made out no more than half a day in advance, since we never know what gifts of food we may receive in the next few hours and maintain no regular supply of staples. Must be ready to cook for an eighty-member family, trusting in the heavenly Father who does not give a stone when one asks Him for bread.

The book is not an account of easy victories, but of daily acts of faith, of seeming crises amazingly overcome. Basilea Schlink writes:

Let us have no wrong conception about miracles. The granting of a petition never follows mechanically, as in a telephone booth when you drop in the second nickel and get a dial tone. To experience miracles means to come in touch with the living and holy God – with the consuming fire which is incompatible with our sins.

The Sisterhood believes that it has proved that 'prayer has absolute prerequisites and that if these are not fulfilled the prayer is impeded'. 'The New Testament,' writes Mother Basilea, 'names several sins which are prayer obstacles. . . . Above all, this includes the transgression of the Ten Commandments, according to Jesus' interpretation in the Sermon on the Mount. In general these are: refusal to forgive (Matthew 6: 15); wrath and doubt (I Timothy 2: 8); all sensuous, passionate behaviour (I Peter 3: 7, 4: 7, 8a); refusal to confess our sins one to another (James 5: 16); stinginess and greediness, because, 'give and it will be given to you; good measure, pressed down, shaken together, running over' (Luke 6: 38); earthly-mindedness, because 'seek first His kingdom and His righteousness, and all these things shall be yours as well' (Matthew 6: 33). 'A decisive obstacle to decisive prayer,' she adds, 'is unrepented and unconfessed sin from which one does not want to depart.'

I have myself, in defiance of my sceptical habit of mind, had many experiences of God's provision not only for myself and my family, but for great enterprises involving a greater number of people and even larger sums than those involved in Dr Muller's work. The work of Moral Re-Armament, with which I have been associated since 1932 and on whose British Council of Management I have been privileged to serve for thirty years, is financed on these same principles. None of its whole-time workers is paid a salary, nor are any of its world-wide enterprises budgeted on the basis of what money is in hand. Both individuals and its travelling forces, which may comprise dozens or hundreds of people on any one mission, undertake what is, as far as they can see, the most daring will of God in the confident hope that money will be provided on time. So far, these hopes have not been disappointed, although, as with Dr Muller and the Sisterhood of Mary, there are many days and moments when the issue seems in doubt.

Such experience has been so common in the history of Christianity as to suggest a universal truth, and this is only one area in which the ordinary person, like myself, can make his own test of faith. Steinmetz, the nineteenth-century scientist and one-time atheist, said before he died: 'The next great discoveries will be made in the realm of the spiritual.' That prophecy has not yet been obviously fulfilled, but it is becoming ever more urgent for man's health, even for his survival, that the necessary experimentation should now take place. 'The power of man,' said Winston Churchill, 'has grown in every sphere except over himself.' Man, who has grown up intellectually, must now grow up morally and spiritually – or perish.

REFERENCES

SIR ALISTER HARDY: 'The Divine Flame' (Collins, 1966), pp. 26, 30, 81, 242–4, 160.

SIR FREDERIC BARTLETT: 'Religion as Experience, Belief, Action' (Oxford University Press, 1950), p. 35.

BARBARA WARD: 'Faith and Freedom' (Hamish Hamilton, 1954), pp. 254-6.

BASILEA SCHLINK: 'Realities' (Oliphants, 1967), pp. 8, 84, 17, 122–3.

13

Commitment for Counter-Attack

by Garth Lean

The story of Christianity in Russia in the last fifty years shows that it has the power to survive in the most unpromising conditions, and may give us the clue of how it can revive throughout the world.

Lenin regarded Christianity as the greatest of all dangers to his ideology. 'Our revolution will never succeed,' he said, 'until the myth of God is removed from the mind of man.' From the first days of the revolution, therefore, persecution of Christians was violent. Untold numbers of clergy of all denominations were shot or condemned to die in labour camps, and a vigorous atheist propaganda was set on foot. It was assumed that in these circumstances, Christianity would die out in a generation, but this did not happen.

Many assume that the Soviet Government accepted this situation, and that, since the celebrated Concordat between the State and the Orthodox Church in 1942, the churches, though reduced, have been protected. 'This,' writes Mr Edward Crankshaw in *The Observer* (18 July 1965) 'is a belief fostered most effectively by certain careerist prelates who do not blush to assure their opposite numbers in the West that religion in Russia today is as free as air and that the State exerts no pressures whatsoever.'

He continues:

In fact, things are worse now than they have been for years past. Krushchev himself initiated a new drive against religion in 1957, which began to have physical effect in 1959. Since then the number of bishops, priests, monasteries and seminaries have been nearly halved, and this operation has been on occasion conducted in a manner reminiscent of the worst days. Monks and nuns have been driven out of their establishments at rifle-point and left to starve or freeze in the forests: those who have sought to succour them intimidated or arrested. Churches have been blown up before the eyes of the faithful, held at bay by police bayonets; distinguished church-men have been tried on trumped-up charges (usually embezzlement) and put away. It is generally believed that the metropolitan Nikolai, who died in a prison hospital, was murdered. This is the mood.

Since religion could not be destroyed, it was infiltrated. Bishops and clergy were given the choice between spying on their people or being dismissed – or worse. Thousands were removed from their parishes. Many more reluctantly, some few eagerly, became Communist agents. So much real Christianity went underground.

The same process took place after the war in the satellite countries, and the story of the underground church in Roumania is told by Pastor Richard Wurm-brand, in his two books, *In God's Underground* and *Tortured for Christ*.

It was in 1944 that a million Russian troops marched into Roumania. Soon afterwards a congress of 4,000 Roumanian priests and pastors of all denominations chose Stalin as their honorary president. Bishops and clergy, one after another, got up and said that Christianity and Communism were fundamentally the same thing.

Wurmbrand and his wife were present. She urged him to get up and speak honestly. 'If I do you lose your husband,' he said. 'I don't wish to have a coward for a husband,' she replied.

Wurmbrand got up and praised not Communism, but Christ. He paid with fourteen years, in two stretches, in prison.

He and others were put to stand in boxes, with nails protruding inwards, so that the slightest movement tore at their flesh. They were continually beaten – or frozen – to the point of death, and then revived. Tens of thousands – children, women and men – have been killed. Yet the spirit of these Christians has not been broken. And they have converted their gaolers as Paul did of old.

Wurmbrand states that even Gheorghiu Dej, the Communist Prime Minister of Roumania, in his last hours surrendered his life to Christ. Two Christians had broken through to him on the steps of a public building and challenged him. They were imprisoned for their pains. But he remembered them as he lay dying.

There are no nominal Christians in the Underground – for it is too dangerous. Every Christian there is a 'winner of souls'. And thousands of the Russian soldiers have been converted by the Christians' fearless witness and the radiance of their lives.

'The *Red Star*,' writes Wurmbrand, 'attacked the Russian Christians, saying, "the worshippers of Christ like to get their greedy claws on everyone". But their shining Christian lives win them the love and respect of their fellow villagers and neighbours. In any village or town, the Christians are the most well-liked, beloved residents. When a mother is too ill to care for her children, it is the Christian mother who comes over and looks after them. When a man is too ill to cut his firewood, it is the Christian man who does it for him. They "live" their Christianity – and when they begin to witness for Christ the people listen and believe – because they have seen Christ in their lives. Since no one but a licensed minister can speak up in a church, the millions of fervent, dedicated Christians in every corner of the communist world win souls, witness and minister in market places, at the village water pumps – anywhere they go. Communist newspapers admit that Christian butchers slip Gospel tracts in the wrapping paper of the meat they sell. The communist press admits that Christians working in places of authority in communist printing houses slip back in late at night, start their presses up and run off a few thousand pieces of Christian literature – and lock up again before the sun rises. The communist press also admits that Christian children in Moscow have received Gospels from 'some source' and then copy portions by hand. The children then place the portions in the overcoat pockets of their teachers, which hang in school closets. The vast body of laymen and laywomen are a very powerful, effective, soul-winning missionary force already in every communist land. . . .

'These millions of dedicated, true and fervent Believers in the lay church have been purified by the very fires of persecution which the communists hoped would destroy them.'

Wurmbrand is not against Communists. He holds to the principle of hating the sin, but loving the sinner. In the West we more often appease the sinner and forgive the sin – the more readily because it is committed against others than ourselves.

'Behind the walls of the Iron Curtain,' he writes, 'the drama, bravery and martyrdom of the Early

Church is happening all over again – now – and the free Church sleeps.'

The Underground Church is committed to win their countries for God. What would happen if Christians in the West had even half their commitment, if every Christian were a changer of men and were prepared to face the consequences? We would only have to face sharp words where they face sharp nails, the intellectual rather than the physical freeze; yet we quail.

Sören Kierkegaard's prediction that 'Christianity may be taken away from Europe as the only way of convincing people of its value' has already been fulfilled in Eastern Europe, where even the Communist ideologists are recognizing that they have failed to produce the new type of man which Communist theory anticipates and which the revolution needs if it is to survive. Christianity can produce such men. The irony is that just as the Communists who do not believe in God are beginning to feel the need of Him, the Western nations, which say they are Christian nations, are losing their faith.

Pastor Wurmbrand has earned the right to speak to the West. He writes: 'I suffer in the West more than I suffered in a communist jail, because now I see with my own eyes the western civilization dying. Oswald Spengler wrote in *Decline of the West*:

You are dying. I see in you all the characteristic stigma of decay. I can prove that your great wealth and your great poverty, your capitalism and your socialism, your wars and your revolutions, your atheism and your pessimism and your cynicism, your immorality, your broken-down marriages, your birth-control, that is bleeding you from the bottom and killing you off at the top in your brains – can

prove to you that these were characteristic marks
of the dying ages of ancient states – Alexandria and
Greece and neurotic Rome.

This was written in 1926. Since then, democracy
and civilization have died already in half of Europe
and even as far as Cuba. The rest of the West sleeps.'

Why do the men of God so often lack the pace and
persistence of the men of anti-God? Christ said: 'Ye
are the salt of the earth: but if the salt has lost its
savour, wherewith shall it be salted?' The context in
the three Gospels makes clear what kind of a person
a 'salted Christian' is. He is persecuted – and rejoices
in it. He puts Christ before his most loved family –
and before life itself. His life and witness is set on a
hill, for everyone to see. He is an infectious case. He is
disciplined ('salted with the fire of the discipline' was
Mahatma Gandhi's favourite text). He takes up his
Cross.

A Western man who in my generation embodied
this commitment as clearly, perhaps, as any other, was
one of those who moved from agnosticism to faith by
an experiment similar to that suggested in the previous
chapter. A hard-boiled, some said malicious, journalist,
at the top of his profession, he one day went to interview a Christian, with the intention of deriding him
and his work, and came away having experimentally
given his life to God. In the next twenty-five years he,
through his plays and books and, most of all, through
personal contact, brought a revival of the spirit to
thousands, perhaps millions, of men in all five contin-
ents. He happened to be a protestant, but at his death,
six cardinals, as well as the leaders of fifteen nations,
recorded their gratitude for what he had done for them
and the world. His name was Peter Howard.

Each man must find his own way to God, and find

from God what part he is meant to play to make Him regnant in the world. But the commitment essential to any Christian reawakening is not in doubt. Peter Howard gave a modern outline of this commitment when he addressed clergy of all denominations in Church House, Westminster:

I am a revolutionary. My life does not belong to myself. I have no preconception of any kind, any day for the rest of my life, where I will go, what I will do or will not do, what I will say or will not say. I want to be used by God if He will use me. . . .

One of the things so wrong in so many of the Christian forces of today is that we think being nice, kind, sweet and owing allegiance to each other is Christian. I love my wife dearly. I have three children and I love them with all my heart, but none of these people is as important to me as Jesus Christ. He comes first in my life. . . .

In my own life, if I am living straight and the maximum God shows me, people change. If people do not change, there is some sin, definite, concrete, which is preventing that happening around me.

If people in their millions are not being changed and won to the truth of Christ, there is something wrong with the way Christians are living their Christianity. If we really wanted, we could find out what it is. Because the God I worship is a God who speaks.

Not every thought I get in my heart comes directly from God. Many of them do not. But I know from experience that if honestly and without preconception I open my heart to God and say, 'What do You want me to do?' then if there is something He wants me to do, He has a way of showing me. God will show us where the sin is if we are not effective. God will give us the answer to it.

I think a Christian revolutionary is meant to be a revolutionary who revolutionizes the situation he is in. Every non-Christian in the world should be saying, 'What are the Christian nations thinking about now? What is their next move? What are they saying? What are they doing?' We ought to be the focus of attention at this time of crisis instead of being a pattern of disunity and ineffectiveness.

I do not criticize youth. We are all to blame. Even some churchmen have become so determined to be 'with it' that they accept secularization as normal and try to make Christ conform to modern compromise instead of struggling, fighting, cleaving with our times until those times conform to the Cross of Christ. Of course, men, whether clerics or otherwise, who live in the grip of secret habits of defeat, cannot and will not tackle a nation in the grip of secularization and compromise.

In one of the last speeches he made before leaving for Peru, where he died, Howard stated:

I feel myself a man of many frailties and much weakness. I hope that before I die I shall have changed out of all recognition and be wholly different tomorrow from what I am today. Just as indeed I am different today from what I was yesterday. But I tell you without soap or sentiment that as I begin each day by listening to God, it is a time of enthralment and fascination that I would not miss.

It is like a great shoal of silver fish flashing through your heart and mind – new ideas for people, fresh approaches to problems, deeper insight into the mood of the times, costly, daily, personal decision that is the price of shifting our force and our nation ahead. I am not much of a fisherman but I try and snatch one or two of those silvery fish as they fly from the Mind of God into the mind of men and women and children like ourselves.

Absolute moral standards are a guide to life. They are like the North Star. It is a fixed point in the sky. It is yet to be recorded that any ship has reached the North Star, but it is true that on every ocean mariners discern from that star where their position is and where they need to head. And absolute moral standards for those who lack faith may be a good starting point if they wish to play their part with all of us in a revolution that will change this country and the world.

For my part, my life is given – and I mean given – to shifting the whole world, Communist and non-Communist alike, to the Cross.

Some of the fruits of Howard's commitment all over the world are documented in a remarkable book, *Peter Howard: Life and Letters,* by his daughter, Anne Wolrige Gordon. It is a book of infinite encouragement because it shows what one man, under God, can achieve. It also shows that a mighty Christian force, like Peter Howard, can be started on his way by someone of no comparable ability and no unusual powers. For I was myself the man whom he approached for the newspaper interview which ended with his making his initial experiment in faith.

REFERENCES

RICHARD WURMBRAND: 'Tortured for Christ' (Hodder & Stoughton, 1967), pp. 68, 15, 25, 96–7, 58, 127, 73–4.
OSWALD SPENGLER: 'The Decline of the West' (Allen & Unwin, 1932).
ANNE WOLRIGE GORDON: 'Peter Howard: Life and Letters' (Hodder & Stoughton, 1969).

NOTE

Prayer as an act of listening:

In the course of an article in *The Times* (23 December, 1968) under the heading 'Prayer as listening, not asking', a contributor wrote:

To me prayer is listening, not asking. And as the voice may be faint and the message both unexpected and unwelcome, it takes much practice and much patience. It is part of this attitude that leads me to treasure the statement of Isaac of Ninevah, one of the saints of the Greek Orthodox Church, who said: 'Prayer is the conversation with God, which takes place in secret.'

When Peter Howard, as in the passages quoted in this chapter, spoke of listening, he referred primarily to a specific time – in his case as early as 4 or 5 a.m. – set aside each day. This is, of course, a very ancient discipline. St Francis de Sales used to say that half an hour's listening each day is a basic minimum, except when you are unusually busy. Then a full hour is necessary.

'God does not stop talking to us any more than the sun stops shining,' said Père Gratry, the saintly French priest of a hundred years ago: 'When shall we listen to Him? In the morning before the distractions and activity of a busy day. How? You write it down. Write it down so that you may preserve the Spirit in you and keep His words.'

14

The Complete Revolution

by Garth Lean

'Secret discipline without worldliness becomes pure ghetto; worldliness without the secret discipline pure boulevard.'
EBERHARD BETHGE.

In a recent Saturday article in *The Times*, headed *The irrelevance of the relevant in the Church*, the Rev M. J. Jackson writes scornfully of what he calls 'the lust for relevance which seems to infect the Churches today'. This 'lust', he states, comes from two sources – first, 'from those with an overwhelming conviction of the truth of Christianity and of its ability to touch and solve every issue' and secondly, 'from those whose eyes are on the rapidly changing world which is slipping away from the Churches' and who feel that 'the Churches must run after it and demonstrate their usefulness'. He accuses the first of these groups of lack of discrimination between the things of God and the things of Caesar; and the second of 'a failure of nerve' which 'ends with the destruction of Christianity, replacing it by utilitarianism and pragmatism'. 'Faith in Christ,' he complains, 'is not for its own sake, but is desirable because it is useful in the solving of a labour dispute and because it works in rehabilitating a racialist.' (*The Times*, 26 November 1968.)

One can sympathize with what Mr Jackson has to

say about loss of nerve. A school of thought exists among theologians in Germany, both East and West, which contends that the work of the Holy Spirit can no longer be seen in the conversion of individuals, but only in such secular movements as the fight for civil rights or Communism. Here 'where developments are most dynamic', it is said God has His own 'incognito way' in the world. This is also the view of many of the 'violent new breed' of clerics in America, to whom we have already referred. Dr Harvey Cox, as we have seen, agrees with Camus that a man can only 'turn his full attention to striving for justice', when he has 'rejected the tyrant God of Christian theology' and become 'a full man' – a process which involves abandoning traditional Christian morality and accepting secularization. Mr Jackson is right to consider such an attitude as sub-Christian, for it is fundamentally atheist.

Mr Jackson, however, appears to go to the other extreme, where all the main fields of social endeavour are abandoned to Caesar and faith in God is conceived as a purely personal matter. Such a conclusion has been reached, by different routes, by two contemporary groups of theologians – the first by a withdrawal into other-worldliness, the second by an acceptance of all the assumptions of secularism. Both attitudes leave the practical world of men empty of God, which would seem to indicate some loss of nerve, or even atheism, as regards large areas of life on this planet.

Professor Henry Drummond, the author of *Natural Law in a Spiritual World*, who, more than any other man, turned Scottish university students away from agnosticism at the end of the last century, struck a wiser balance in his address, *The Programme of Christianity*. He wrote:

Next to losing the sense of a personal Christ, the worst evil that can befall a Christian is to have no sense of anything else. To grow up in a complacent belief that God has no business in this great groaning world of human beings except to attend to a few saved souls is the negation of all religion. The first great epoch in a Christian's life, after the awe and wonder of its dawn, is when there breaks into his mind that Christ has a purpose for mankind, a purpose beyond him and his needs, beyond the churches and their creeds, beyond Heaven and its saints – a purpose which embraces every man and woman born, every kindred and nation formed, which regards not their spiritual good alone but their welfare in every part, their progress, their health, their work, their wages, their happiness in this present world.

It is in the framework of this purpose that the importance of solving a labour dispute or rehabilitating a racialist – to quote Mr Jackson's examples – lies. Such social cures are not substitutes for faith in Christ, but the natural byproduct of living out that faith in the world of men. Thus, most authorities attribute to the Evangelical Revival such social reforms as the abolition of slavery and the slave trade, factory and prison reform, and the fact that the British Labour Movement grew up through the nineteenth century with a mainly Christian, rather than a Marxist, philosophy. The Wesleys, who initiated that reawakening, certainly spoke out against slavery and other social ills, but their prime task was preaching that faith which, as the great ecclesiastical historian, J. H. Overton, wrote, 'made the selfish man self-denying, the discontented happy, the worldling spiritually-minded, the drunkard sober, the sensual chaste, the liar truthful, the thief honest, the proud humble, the godless godly, the thriftless thrifty'. Such changed men become the foot soldiers of reform. And their leaders – Wilberforce, Shaftesbury, Keir Hardie and the rest – found their incentive in a similar change. All could say with Keir Hardie, the founder of the Parliamentary Labour Party, 'I myself found in the Christianity of Christ the inspiration which first drove me into this movement and which has carried me on in it.'

The 'new theologians' would have us believe that no such changes take place today, that God does not intervene in men's lives or in the events of the present world. To see how wide of the mark they are, one has only to read M. Gabriel Marcel's book *Fresh Hope for the World* in which that distinguished philosopher sets out changes as remarkable as those seen in any other age. Among the 'decisive encounters' which he records – encounters which effected 'not a subjective change, but a radical change of personality' – are those of a steel industrialist, a national trades union secretary and the General Secretary of the Socialist Women, all of his native France; a founder of the Norwegian Communist Party, a Ruhr miner whose conversion began in a Soviet prison camp, an African chief, a Canadian industrialist, some Brazilian dockers and a Japanese student leader. The effect of their change on their industries and the wider problems of their nations are too extensive to describe here, but can be read in M. Marcel's book, where he writes of having 'irrefutable evidence', for example, that they had 'a direct impact on the political life of various countries in the Far East and that statesmen – such as the President of the Philippines, the Prime Minister of Japan and so on – were directly influenced'.

The original title of M. Marcel's book was *Un Changement d'Espérance à la Rencontre du Réarmement Moral*, and I know all those in it and have observed 'the radical changes of personality' which he attributes to them. Other Christians will bear witness to the reality of changes they have observed in people within their own experience. Evidence from every source is needed, if the practical atheism of those who believe, with Dr Altizer, that 'no responsible person can any longer experience God' is to be refuted.

'Christianity,' the Archbishop of Canterbury told some students at the London School of Economics 'is the most revolutionary creed in the world because it seeks a revolution in man.' (*The Times*, 21 November, 1968.) The distinctive thing is that it not only seeks it, but achieves it. Most secular revolutionaries, also, seek a new type of man, but with less success. Shulubin, the old Communist in Alexander Solzhenitsyn's *Cancer Ward*, says, 'We thought it was enough to change the mode of production and immediately people would change as well. But did they change? The hell they did! They didn't change a bit.' The Norwegian Communist leader of whom M. Marcel writes confirmed this view. He told me that the new and better man which was expected to emerge naturally with the establishment of Communism, was the 'unfinished business' of every Moscow conference which he attended. Certainly, Stalin himself who presided at those conferences neither exemplified the new man – nor knew how to change others. Instead, he liquidated them in their millions.

The student revolutionaries of Europe, as we have seen, seek 'a new human being, unexploited, creative, spontaneous, uninhibited, social' – and hope that he, like the new society of which they dream, will emerge spontaneously out of the ruins of the society they hope to destroy. Yet they have not convinced their own generation that they have produced the kind of human being who can guarantee that the liberty they speak of will survive their revolution. A party of young Czechs who visited Rudi Dutschke in Berlin in the spring of 1967 reported back: 'There was no contact. People like Dutschke think they are talking about revolutionary democracy. If they had their way it would lead to Stalinism again.' (*Weekend Telegraph*, 6 December 1968.)

Similarly, Franz Fanon, the black psychiatrist from Martinique whose book *The Wretched of the Earth* is said to be the bible of the Black Power movement, cried: 'For Europe, for ourselves and for humanity, comrades, we must turn a new leaf, we must work out new concepts, and try and set afoot a new man.' 'These are brave and challenging words,' commented Dr Martin Luther King. 'But the problem is that Fanon and those who quote his words are seeking to "work out new concepts" and "set afoot a new man" with a willingness to imitate old concepts of violence. Is not there a basic contradiction here? Violence has been the inseparable twin of materialism, the hallmark of its grandeur and misery. This is the one thing about modern civilization that I do not care to imitate.'

No one, it is said, is more reactionary than the man who wants to change the world, but is unwilling to change himself – except, perhaps, the man who does not want to change the world at all. And over against the revolutionaries and pseudo-revolutionaries of our day are the status quo men, millions of them, who wish to change nothing because they are comfortably placed as they are. Mr Jackson, in his *Times* article, would appear to agree with them. He states that 'the lust for relevance . . . is fathered by the spirit of the age which has absorbed the Marxist fiction that it is the duty of philosophy not to understand the world but to change it'. Would he contend that those who were enjoined to pray 'Thy Kingdom come, Thy will be done on earth as it is in heaven' have no duty to try and change the world? Such a prayer, if accepted as a commitment rather than repeated as a pious drone or a casual insincerity, is a declaration of revolution more fundamental than anything Marx ever wrote.

Whether we will succeed in changing the world is not the point. 'Let us raise a standard to which the wise and honest may repair,' George Washington said of a great, but lesser cause. 'The event is in the hand of God.'

One schism which faces Christians today, just as the Churches are drawing together, is within every church. On the one hand is a ghetto philosophy which keeps personal faith intact, but does little or nothing to equip and remotivate us to save the lives of millions of people faced with tyranny or starvation. On the other hand is a social programme, with only remote Christian antecedents, which is turning to that revolutionary violence which Christ repudiated for His own disciples.

This, like other statements examined in the next chapter, is a fake alternative. The complete revolution is one which begins by transforming the self-centred motives of the individual and goes on to change his relationships with all men, everywhere. It is a programme of social, national and international change, all based on personal change – the greatest of all revolutions whereby the Cross of Christ transforms the world.

REFERENCES

DR HARVEY COX: 'The Secular City' (Macmillan, New York, 1966), p. 72.

HENRY DRUMMOND: 'The Greatest Thing in the World and 21 other Addresses' (Collins, 1930), pp. 65–66.

J. H. OVERTON: 'The Evangelical Revival in the Eighteenth Century' (Longmans, 1886), p. 131.

KEIR HARDIE: 'J. Keir Hardie' by William Stewart (Cassell, 1921), p. 303.

GABRIEL MARCEL: 'Fresh Hope for the World' (Longmans, 1960), pp. 5, 3 etc.

SHULUBIN: From an Extract from 'Cancer Ward', volume 2, by Alexander Solzhenitsyn (Bodley Head, 1969), printed in *The Times Saturday Review* on 22 February, 1969.

FRANZ FANON: Quoted by Dr Martin Luther King in 'Chaos or Community' (Hodder & Stoughton, 1968), pp. 65–6, where Dr King's comment also appears.

15
A Job Waiting to be Done

An effective Christian counter-attack will not neglect the exposure of a fashionable fallacy, the fallacy of the fake alternative. A fake alternative is a statement which implies that we must choose between two ideals or two policies, both of which not only can be but often should be simultaneously attempted, as, for instance, 'Be good, sweet maid and let who will be clever.' Some sweet maids are both good and clever.

Fake alternatives are popular with those who are depressed by the exacting demands of the Christian code and who therefore insist that 'charity is more important than chastity', as if the unchaste were invariably charitable and the chaste invariably uncharitable.

A less explicit example of the fake alternative is the implication that if we love our neighbour we need not worry about whether we also love God, and indeed need not even remember that our Lord said, 'Thou shalt love the Lord thy God with all thy heart, and with all thy soul, and with all thy mind. This is the first and great commandment. And the second is like unto it, Thou shalt love thy neighbour as thyself.' (St Matthew XXII: 37.)

It is, of course, tempting to de-emphasize the duty to love God, for Christ associated the love of God not only with love of one's neighbour but also with keeping His commandments. 'If ye love me, keep my commandments' (St John XIV: 15), a precept which is naturally rejected not only by secularists but also by those modernist disciples of the computerized Christianity which replaces the Ten Commandments by the Ten Suggestions.

Christians who are more anxious to conciliate than to convert the world often rationalize their reluctance to make an effective contribution to Christian action by such fake alternatives as 'It is living Christianity rather than talking about it which makes converts.' Living it is, of course, essential. Justin Martyr, who died *c.* A.D. 165, wrote of 'many pagans who have changed their violent and tyrannical dispositions, being overcome either by the constancy which they witnessed in the lives of their Christian neighbours or by the honesty of those believers with whom they transacted business' – and that process continues to this day. But the great missionaries have both lived *and* talked about Christianity, and those who deprecate talking about Christianity are not invariably successful in converting atheists by the examples of their lives. Of Livingstone, H. M. Stanley wrote, 'If I had been with him any longer I would have been compelled to become a Christian, and he never spoke to me about it at all.' This then was one of Livingstone's failures, but he made many converts among those who were not only influenced by the example of his life but also by his spoken tribute to Christianity.

Courage is the basic virtue, and many of these fake alternatives are rationalizations of the cowardice which is mainly responsible for the decline of Christianity. Christ provoked hate as well as love, and warned His followers that they too would be hated. Too many Christians are anxious to substitute a Church appeaser for the Church Militant. 'Dialogue,' we are often assured by intimidated Christians, 'does more good than controversy,' but controversy cannot be excluded from any worthwhile 'dialogue' between a Christian and a secularist who rejects the supernatural. Is it, indeed, as Karl Barth asked, 'so certainly right to allow dialogue with the world to take precedence over proclamation to the world'?

Intimidated Christians are unconsciously influenced by a misinterpretation of democracy, the belief in the infallibility of Gallup Popery. Gallup Poll Christians are depressed by the decline of Christianity, and much that they write is unconsciously influenced by the kind of considerations which influence a political party which has been thrown out of office: how can the party policy be revised to regain the desired majority.

For the authentic Christian the Gallup Poll is no criterion of the truths of Christianity, but is often a useful criterion of the effectiveness of Christian publicity. Yes, publicity, for our task is to get the Gospel, that is, the 'good news', across to the public. Inadequate use is made of television, that most effective medium of propaganda. In our secular society the great majority are not agnostics but indifferentists. If they are not interested, that is less a reflection on them than on their Christian fellow-citizens who have made so little attempt to interest them, for example, in the Christian solution of the problem in which no intelligent person could fail to be interested: Is man nothing but the by-product of material agencies and doomed to ultimate extinction in the grave, or has the individual any ultimate significance?

There are, of course, others who are primarily interested in the Christian solution to social problems or to their personal difficulties or the difficulties of someone for whom they care. The Christian approach to the non-Christian is a problem of communication

– how to meet the personal needs of each individual. The Christian must be able to meet those who claim to be rationalists on their own ground and also to help those who seek liberation from the tyranny of some particular sin. In the eighteenth century Bishop Butler who refuted the Deists with a rational defence of Christianity, and John Wesley, whose major theme was sin and salvation, both made an essential contribution to the great Revival.

'There are,' writes Professor William Barclay, 'two revelations in Christianity – the revelation of God and the revelation of ourselves. No man ever really sees himself until he sees himself in the presence of Christ; and then he is appalled at the sight of himself. There is another way of putting it – Christianity begins with a sense of sin. It begins with the sudden realization that life as we are living it will not do. We awake to ourselves and we awake to the need of God.'

Our task today is not only to the reconversion of countries once at least nominally Christian, but also to prevent the perversion of those who are still Christians, if only borderline Christians. To the solution of these basic problems it is not only the great saints like St Bernadette and the Curé d'Ars, but also the great apologists such as G. K. Chesterton and C. S. Lewis who have made an essential contribution.

'If Christ be not risen, then is our preaching vain, and your faith is also vain.' (I Corinthians XV: 14.) If our counter-attack is to succeed, we must take due note of Pauline priorities. The moral and the secular consequences of accepting Christianity are of immense importance, but why should anybody attempt to practise the exacting Christian code if Christ was not more than a Galilean mystic whose hopes perished with him on the Cross? If Christ be not risen, and if we cannot convince the world that Christ rose from the dead, then is our preaching vain. It is usual for priests to preach on the Resurrection on Easter Sunday, but how many priests and how many ministers of religion ever give their congregation any reason for believing in the Resurrection? Christians should, in the words of St Peter, 'be ready always to give an answer to every man that asketh you a reason of the hope that is in you'. (I Peter III: 15.)

We are faced today by a concerted and organized attempt to eliminate what little is left of the Christian influence in the Western world, but there is as yet no attempt to organize a counter-attack. Even in private conversation we should never restrict ourselves to defending Christianity against attack, we should also expose the irrationality of all varieties of pure secularism.

There are many different methods of approaching the non-Christian, just as there are many different medical treatments for different patients. Two such approaches are described in this book. A Christian may specialize in the approach which he finds easiest, and avoid another approach because he fears that he could not do justice to it, but to imply that the individual is compelled to choose between different methods of approach to the unconverted is an example of fake alternatives. The Christian who is an expert at stating the rational case for Christianity would probably have more hope of success if he could reinforce the rational argument by a more personal and experimental approach, and all Christian apologists, whatever method they favour, are even more effective if they can give a reason for the hope that is in them when asked to justify their conviction that Christianity is true, and that Christ was what He claimed to be and did rise from the dead.

What is contemptible is the all too prevalent attempt by intimidated Christians to deprecate any attempt to convert secularists to Christianity. Such Christians fear that a vigorous counter-attack on the secular basis of our society might make things uncomfortable for Christians at large.

Characteristic of non-combatant Christianity was the reaction not of all but of one vocal member of a University Ecumenical society to which A.L. lectured. He had asked the secretary to arrange for a debate between him and a secular 'Humanist'. 'Oh, that would provoke hostility,' was the reply. Dynamic Christianity has, one must admit, a tendency to provoke hostility.

Dwight Moody, the American evangelist, was once accosted in an English train by this type of Christian.

'You're Moody, aren't you?' he exclaimed. 'I don't like your methods.'

'I'm not too satisfied with them myself,' said Moody. 'How do you make people into Christians?'

'Oh, I don't do that sort of thing,' was the reply.

'Well,' said Moody, 'on the whole I prefer the way I try to do it, to the way you don't.'

Christianity will revive when the consequences of repudiating God, which are now so apparent, force men to turn to the only remedy for their ills, the return to God, and when the number of those who are prepared to dedicate their lives to the conversion of the world is greatly increased. In this great battle today, as in the beginnings of Christianity, different Christians will have different vocations, 'having then gifts', as St Paul said to the earliest missionaries, 'differing according to the grace that is given to us'. Thus we all have a job waiting to be done.

Index

Ali, Tariq, 36
Altizer, Dr, 88, 89, 164
Amis, Kingsley, 25, 26, 28
Anderson, Perry, 62-3
Apollinaire, Guillaume, 20, 21
Argyle, Malcolm, Q.C., 41
Artaud, 61
Ascherson, Neal, 59
Auden, W. H., 19, 35
Ayer, Prof., A. J., 118, 137

Back, Dr Nathan, 43
Bacon, Alice, 41, 42
Baldwin, James, 21, 22
Barclay, Prof. William, 77, 171
Barth, Karl, 170
Bartlett, Sir Frederic, 139, 142
Bateson, Dr, 105
Bell, Colin, 29
Bennett, Dr, John, 88
Bethge, Eberhard, 85, 86, 160
Black Dwarf, The, 62
Blackham, Harold, 71
Blamires, Harry, 89, 102
Bonhoeffer, Dietrich, 83-6
Bosanquet, Mary, 85, 89
Boyle, Sir Edward, 26
Braun, Prof. Herbert, 87
British Medical Journal, 44
Broad, Prof. C. D., 101
Brodie, Ian, 50
Brophy, Brigid, 23
Brown, Dr Felix, 41
Budenz, Louis, 3, 125

Bultmann, Rudolf, 87
Bury, Prof. J. B., 6
Butler, Bishop, 171

Callaghan, James, 35
Camps, Prof F. E., 37
Camus, Albert, 83, 161
Canterbury, Archbishop of, 164
Caruana, Dr Salvino, 39
Chesterton, G. K., 19, 74, 124, 137, 171
Christianity Today, 81
Churchill, Winston, 149
Clark, Colin, 73
    Eric, 6
    Ronald, 126, 134
Clifford, Lord, 31, 32
Cogley, John, 87
Cohen, Dr M. M., 43
Cohn-Bendit, D., 53
Connolly, Cyril, 18-20, 22, 53, 67
Conquest, Robert, 130
Coulton, G. C., 136
Cox, Dr Harvey, 82, 83, 84, 161
Crankshaw, Edward, 150
Crawford, Margaret, 122
Crick, Dr F. H. C., 72-3
Critchley, Julian, 70
Crossman, Richard, 30

Daily Express, 37, 39, 51, 73
Daily Telegraph, 14
Davey, Richard, 63
Dej, Gheorghiu, 152

Devlin, Lord, 70
Drummond, Henry, 161-2
Durant, Dr Will, 22
Dutschke, Rudi, 165
Dwight, Prof. Thomas, 107, 127

Encounter, 66, 75
English, David, 51
Epstein, Brian, 36

Fanon, Franz, 165
Farrer, Dr Austin, 72
Fielder, Leslie, 21
Findlay, Stephen, 94
Fisk, Trevor, 58
Fletcher, Dr Joseph, 79, 80, 84
Flew, Anthony, 96
Fryer, Peter, 66-8
Fuller, Roy, 68

Gandhi, Mahatma, 155
Gifford, Lord, 138
Ginsberg, Allen, 36
Girodias, Maurice, 27
Gratry, Père, 159
Guardian, The, 25, 26

Haldane, Prof. J. B. S., 98, 108,
    122, 125-30, 134, 136
Hammarskjøld, Dag, 47
Hansford Johnson, Pamela, 23,
    26, 47, 66, 68
Hardy, Sir Alister, 96, 99, 101,
    102, 105, 106, 108, 138, 139
Harrington, Dr J. A., 40
Harris, Lou, 15
Haskard, Oliver, 32
Hefner, Hugh, 78
Herbert, Sir Edwin, 135
Hogg, Quintin, 44, 54, 62, 63
Hollis, Christopher, 121, 132
Howard, Peter, 155-8, 159
Hume, David, 100
Huxley, Sir Julian, 95, 106, 127,
    136
    T. H., 17, 18, 19, 71, 100-1,
    103-4
Ilichev, L. F., 129

Inge, Dean, 6
International Times, 66-7
Isis, 65

Jackson, Rev. M. J., 160-2, 165-6
Jeger, Lena, 25
Joad, Prof. C. E. M., 3, 97, 111,
    120, 125
Johnson, Paul, 74

Keith, Sir Arthur, 107
Kennedy, Senator Robert, 51,
    52-3, 81
Kierkegaard, Soren, 6, 154
Kilmuir, Lord, 30, 32
King, Rev. Martin Luther, 54,
    165
Knight, Margaret, 71
Knox, Monsignor Ronald, 117,
    143
Koestler, Arthur, 75
Krutch, Joseph Wood, 19-22

Lancet, The, 37
Leach, Dr Edmund, 11, 72, 74
Lecomte Du Noüy, Dr, 103
Lemoine, Paul, 106
Levy, Michael, 24
Lewis, C. S., 171
Longford, Lord, 31, 32
Lowell, Robert, 20
Lyons, Eugene, 131

MacDougall, Prof. William, 93
Malraux, André, 20, 23, 61, 62,
    70, 74
Marcel, Gabriel, 163-4
Marcuse, Herbert, 58, 59, 61, 62
Marlowe, John, 48
Mascall, Prof. E. L., 1, 102
Medawar, Sir Peter, 126
Moody, Dwight, 173
Mores, Dr, 118
Morison, Frank, 116
Mount, Anson, 79, 80
Muggeridge, Malcolm, 25, 77,
    146
Muller, George, 144-5
Murray, Sir Gilbert, 94
—, J. C., 14

Nature, 105
New Left, The, 62
New Statesman, The, 25, 74
New York Times, The, 52, 87

Observer, The, 6, 28, 29, 42, 49,
    54, 55, 59, 70, 71, 150
Observer Colour Magazine, 29,
    49, 64, 71
Orwell, George, 133
Osborne, Charles, 24
—, John, 21
Overton, J. H., 162

Panikkar, K. M., 12
Pares, Sir Bernard, 130
Paton, Prof. W. D. M., 42, 45
Paul, His Holiness Pope, 14
Phillips, Canon J. B., 113, 114,
    120, 123
Playboy, 78, 79, 80
Pratt, J. G., 94, 95

Ramsay, Dr Paul, 15
Reich, Wilhelm, 59-60, 61
Reinke, 104
Reisman, David, 63
Reith, Lord, 11
Renan, Ernest, 18, 19, 23
Reston, James, 52, 53
Rhine, Prof. J. B., 93-6, 101, 102
Robinson, Dr John, 80

Salmon, Dr, 112
Saturday Evening Post, 43
Saturday Review, 20
Schlink, Basilea, 146-8
Scott, Peter, 59
Serge, Victor, 131
Seward, Sir Albert, 104-5
Sidgwick, Mrs Henry, 94
Shields, Robert, 64
Silone, Ignazio, 75
Sjøvall, Dr E., 30
Smyth, Edward, 136
Soal, Dr S. G., 95, 101
SOMA, 35-41
Sontag, Susan, 21
Spengler, Oswald, 154

Stacey, Rev. Nicholas, 4-5
Stafford-Clark, Dr David, 36, 38
Steiner, Dr George, 60-1
Stevas, St John, 25
Storr, Dr Anthony, 36, 38-9, 63
Stransky, Father Thomas, 14
Streeter, Dr B. H., 33
Strauss, D. F., 112
Students Today, 58-9
Sunday Telegraph, 35
Sunday Times, The, 19, 27, 61

Tablet, The, 137
Teresa, Mother, 145
Thomas, George, 30
Time Magazine, 14, 15, 49, 51,
    78, 81
Times, The, 13, 31, 32, 36, 37-8,
    40, 41, 45, 53, 54, 61, 63,
    64, 70, 72, 74, 130, 160, 164,
    165
Toynbee, Prof. Arnold, 94
    Philip, 1
Tschernavin, Prof., 130

Updike, John, 48

Vosper, Dennis, 29

Waldron, Brian, 53
Ward, Barbara, 140, 143
Watson, Dr J. B., 104, 117
Weekend Telegraph, 29, 165
Wells, H. G., 106, 128, 133
Wesley, John, 1-2, 162, 171
West, Dr D. J., 94
Whitehead, Prof. A. N., 130
Whitehorn, Katharine, 28, 29, 49
Williams, Prof. Glanville, 32
Willams, Jay, 53
Wilson, Dr Bryan, 4, 13, 14
Wolman, Dr Benjamin, 64
Wolrige Gordon, Anne, 158
Woodcock, George, 62, 63
Wootton, Baroness, 25, 36
Wurmbrand, Pastor Richard,
    151-5

Young, Wayland, 25